Contents

Introduction

The purpose of this book is to help secure the loan that is right for you. There are no good or bad loans—your circumstances determine how much you will have to pay in fees and interest. If a high-interest, high-fee loan is the best you can get, you got a good loan. Only if you pay more than necessary is it truly a bad loan.

This book covers the major loan options available to borrowers, and describes who will benefit most from each. When you find the type of loan that fits your circumstances, you can be confident that you are going to get the best loan for you.

Finding the best lender for each type of loan is also discussed. You will learn the things you should do on your own, as well as the questions you should ask your lender or mortgage broker before agreeing to accept a loan. You do not want to find the best type of loan and then deal with a lender that overcharges you.

Different types of mortgage loans emphasize different areas of the loan. For example, one may be designed to make the monthly payment as low as possible. Another may feature the lowest possible interest rate. Still another may be attractive because of the low down payment. There are many variations.

However, all loans have certain things in common. The borrower must make a monthly payment, pay interest on the money borrowed, and pay back the loan at some future date. Because of these common elements, there may be some repetition in describing and examining each type.

When you think that you are reading something that you have read before, you will be partially correct.

Unless specified, all information refers to loans made by so-called *institutional lenders*, such as banks, savings and loans, and credit unions. Loans made by individuals, such as sellers of property, are covered separately.

Risk and Profit

Before getting into the specific types of mortgages, it is important to understand the basics of mortgage lending. The two intertwined factors that control the lending industry are risk and profit.

Risk determines the cost to the borrower. The higher the risk to the lender, the higher the cost to the borrower. If the borrower is willing to take on more risk, the lender will reduce the cost of the loan. Cost can be in the form of the interest rate, fees, or both.

There are the obvious risks. A borrower with poor credit, marginally acceptable income, high debt, or little or no down payment creates a higher risk that the loan will not be repaid. A borrower with any of these problems will, and should expect to, pay more to borrow money.

Another type of risk is in the stability of the mortgage interest rate. If the borrower insists that the interest rate on the mortgage never increase, called a *fixed interest rate mortgage* (FIRM), the borrower will pay more for the loan. This type of loan puts all the risk of future higher interest rates on the lender. If the borrower is willing to accept the risk that the interest rate may increase, called an *adjustable rate mortgage* (ARM), the borrower will pay less for the original interest rate of the loan. As you read on, you will see how much risk you, as a borrower, should shift from the lender to yourself is a difficult decision.

Lenders believe loans that put them at greater risk should return a higher *profit* than safer loans. This seems reasonable. The borrower's job is to find the lender willing to take the smallest amount of profit for the particular loan that the buyer wants. Again, not an easy task.

Profit for the lender comes from interest, points, and other fees. If a mortgage broker is involved, his or her fee can be paid by either the

borrower or the lender. If paid by the lender, the borrower then pays a higher interest rate to enable the lender to recoup the money.

The second way that lenders make more profit is that some loan programs are simply more profitable than others. This means that a lender may try to sell you a loan that is a good deal for the lender, but not for you. Since lenders know much more about loan programs than borrowers, you start off with a major disadvantage. You are reading this book to try to lessen the odds against you and find the mortgage loan that you want, not the one the lender wants you to have.

Getting a general understanding of the mortgage industry, as well as specific knowledge of the loans currently being offered by most lenders, should give you the ability to avoid the hype and concentrate on the truly important features of the loan you are being offered. Once you can do this, you can get a mortgage loan that will be best suited to your situation.

Chapter 1

What is a Mortgage?

In simple terms, a *mortgage* is putting up real property (real estate) to secure a loan. This means if you fail to meet the terms of the mortgage, the lender can sell your house through a process called *foreclosure* to get back the money borrowed. The most common failure to fulfill the terms is to fall behind on the agreed-upon payments.

Terminology associated with mortgages is often used incorrectly. In fact, the incorrect usage of many terms associated with mortgages has become so common, they are accepted as correct. However, the result of this practice is that when the correct term is used, many are left wondering what is being said. You may be familiar with many common terms associated with the mortgage process, but you also need to know the technical (correct) terms.

A mortgage is a two-party document—the *mortgagor* (borrower) gives the mortgage, and the *mortgagee* (lender) lends the money. Most people incorrectly say that they are going to "get" a mortgage. The expression has become so common, everyone knows that someone who says it is trying to borrow—not lend—money.

> **From the Expert**
>
> The law classifies your property. Real property, also called *real estate*, consists of land and those things affixed to land, such as buildings, fences, trees, in-ground swimming pools, or any other attachment. *Personal property* is generally classified as all property that is not real property. Mortgages only cover real property.

The second term that is misused is *pledge*. To pledge something is to deliver physical possession of it, as if getting a loan from a pawnshop. When you do not give up possession, you *hypothecate* the property—you do not pledge it. Since pledge is a simpler word that hypothecate, it is commonly used—even though not technically correct.

How are Mortgages Structured?

There are two general ways that mortgages are structured. The structure affects how the foreclosure procedures are performed should you not make your mortgage payments. In so-called *title theory* states, the lender owns the property and deeds it back to the borrower when the loan is repaid. When a person is asked if he or she owns or rents, and responds that the bank owns it, in a title theory state they are technically correct. However, the home owner has a lot more rights to the property than anyone else, including the bank. In *lien theory* states, the borrower owns the property and the lender has a *lien* on it. The title theory states are more commonly found in the eastern part of the country, with more lien theory states in the western United States.

In either a title theory or lien theory state, the general effect is the same. The lender's rights in the property are only for the purpose of security. If the borrower abides by the terms of the note and mortgage, the lender has no right to interfere with the borrower's use and enjoyment of the property.

From the Expert

A *lien* is the interest a creditor has in your property. It secures the debt and gives the creditor the legal right to take your property if you fail to meet the terms of your debt agreement. A lien is not a bad thing in and of itself, because without the protection liens give lenders, far fewer loans would be made.

NOTE: *A third theory, which is a hybrid of the two, is used in some states. It is called the* intermediary theory. *In an intermediary theory state, the borrower has title, but the lender can take it if there is a default. Again, the general effect is the same.*

The differences in the theories may become important when the borrower fails to abide by the terms of the mortgage loan. The foreclosure process does vary from state to state, with some state laws being more favorable to the borrower and some to the lender. Since state laws control the real property located within that state, every person must follow the laws of his or her particular state.

When the loan is repaid, the lien is released. As a practical matter, it comes down to this—if you make your payments, you will eventually have ownership of your home free and clear. If you fail to make your payments, you will lose your home through foreclosure.

In some states, a *deed of trust*—also called a *trust deed*—is used in place of a mortgage. A deed of trust accomplishes the same goal as the mortgage, but it is structured differently. The deed of trust is a three-party document. The borrower is called the *trustor* and the lender is called the *beneficiary*. The deed of trust is not made out directly to the beneficiary, but is instead given to a third party called a *trustee*. The trustee acts in only two situations. If the deed of trust is satisfied and the loan paid off, the trustee issues a *reconveyance* to the trustor, releasing the lien. If the terms of the agreement are not met (default), the trustee acts for the beneficiary (lender) to sell the property. Chapter 20 discusses this situation and how to avoid it.

> **From the Expert**
> A *reconveyance* is a legal term for returning something, such as the deed for your home to you.

The term *mortgage* will be used for both mortgages and deeds of trust.

Deed of Trust States:

Alaska	Nevada
Arizona	North Carolina
California	Virginia
Mississippi	Washington, DC
Missouri	

Mortgage States:

Alabama	Minnesota
Arkansas	New Hampshire
Connecticut	New Jersey
Delaware	New Mexico
Florida	New York
Hawaii	North Dakota
Indiana	Ohio
Kansas	Oregon
Kentucky	Pennsylvania
Louisiana	Rhode Island
Maine	South Carolina
Massachusetts	Vermont
Michigan	Wisconsin

States that use both Deeds of Trust and Mortgages:

Colorado	Oklahoma
Georgia	Oregon
Idaho	Tennessee
Illinois	Texas
Iowa	Utah
Maryland	Wyoming
Montana	Washington
Nebraska	West Virginia

A mortgage is used in two different ways. One is to borrow money to buy real estate, and the other is to borrow money against real estate already owned by the borrower. In some areas of the country, there is a major difference between the two if the property is foreclosed upon. This is discussed further in Chapter 20.

Promissory Notes

When you sign all the documents that go along with taking out a mortgage, you will also sign what is called a *promissory note* (also referred to simply as a *note*). This is the document that sets out the terms of the loan, and as the name implies, is your promise to repay the money. The mortgage is the document that puts up your real estate to secure repayment. In other words, the promissory note describes how much you are borrowing and the terms of the loan, while the mortgage is what gives the bank the right to take your home if you do not live up to what you agree to do in the promissory note. It is common for the mortgage to restate all the terms of the note, making the documents sometimes look very similar. However, they have very distinct purposes.

The reason the note is so important is because it is a *negotiable instrument*. Negotiable instruments are what make the system work. A buyer of a negotiable instrument, as long as the procedure is done properly, becomes a *holder in due course*. The point behind a holder in due course is that once the loan has been sold, you may be stuck with it—even if you did not fully understand the terms or there were irregularities because of a dishonest original lender. Later, a worksheet is provided that will help you find the best loan for your situation. (see p.167.)

The rules and court cases surrounding what rights a holder in due course have are numerous and complicated. Negotiable instruments and the rights of a holder in due course of a negotiable instrument give lenders a level of security that they will be repaid and can continue to make financial transactions. This is so important because most loans are sold to other financial institutions in what is called the *secondary market*. (See Chapter 2 for a discussion of the secondary market players.) Selling loans allows for a continuous flow of money, giving primary lenders the ability to keep making loans to individual borrowers.

> ### From the Expert
> Never sign the note and mortgage unless you understand all the terms.

The Mortgage Industry

There is a long list of lenders who make loans using a mortgage for security. They include government agencies, lending institutions (such as banks and mortgage bankers), credit unions, finance companies, mortgage brokers that arrange loans, insurance companies, and even individuals.

There are two types of lenders. The *primary lender* is the one you will deal with. This may be a local bank or other financial institution that meets with you and *originates* your loan. After your transaction is completed, your primary lender can either keep the loan or sell it on the secondary market. If your lender keeps the loan, it is called a *portfolio loan*.

Entities that buy existing loans on the secondary mortgage market may be pension funds, for example, or even primary lenders that have money but cannot originate enough loans. The largest buyers are government agencies or quasi-government agencies—private companies originally created by Congress.

Why Would a Primary Lender Sell a Loan?

Primary lenders make money on the fees you pay when the loan is made and on the interest they collect over the life of your loan. However, if you have a 30-year loan, it will take the primary lender thirty years to make all its money. This ties up money the lender has available to make loans into one property and borrower for the life of the loan. If the primary lender sells the loan, it makes an immediate profit on its money and gives the lender money to continue making other loans.

A primary lender can also make money on *servicing* the loan it sells. This means that the primary lender still sends your monthly statement and collects the money, but then forwards it to the company that bought the loan. In other words, the primary lender acts as an administrator of sorts for a loan it sells, and then charges a fee for that service.

Will You Know if Your Loan is Sold?

You may or may not ever know whether your loan has been sold. If your primary lender is still servicing the loan, you will not know. If the buyer of your loan is servicing it or uses a different servicing agent, you will get a notice that your mortgage has been sold, and you should make future payments to the buyer or buyer's servicing agent.

Regardless of whether your loan is sold or not, the terms of your loan will not change. It is not something that you need to worry about. People often think that their payments are going to increase or their interest rate will rise if their loan is sold, but that is not true.

Who Buys These Loans?

The two organizations that buy the most loans are the Federal National Mortgage Association, known as *Fannie Mae,* and the Federal Home Loan Mortgage Corporation, better known as *Freddie Mac.* They are private companies that began as government agencies.

The following is how Freddie Mac describes itself.

> *Freddie Mac is a stockholder-owned corporation chartered by Congress in 1970 to keep money flowing to mortgage lenders in support of home-ownership and rental housing. Freddie Mac purchases single-family and multifamily residential mortgages and mortgage-related securities, which it finances primarily by issuing mortgage pass through*

> *securities and debt instruments in the capital markets. By doing so, we*
> *ultimately help homeowners and renters get lower housing costs and*
> *better access to home financing.*

This means it gets its money by selling instruments that are types of bonds on Wall Street. The mortgage rates are the rate of return on the mortgage backed securities, and the mortgages secure the debt. You can buy a mortgage-backed security, creating a big circle that keeps the money flowing.

The government agency Government National Mortgage Association (*Ginnie Mae*) is also involved in the secondary market. Ginnie Mae doesn't buy loans or issue mortgage-backed securities. Its role is to *guarantee* investors their payments on mortgage-backed securities, reducing the risks associated with these investments. Less risk generally means more people are willing to invest — keeping more money in the system so more loans can be made.

In order to make the system run smoothly, the secondary market participants set out guidelines for primary lenders. If the primary lender *conforms* (follows the guidelines in making the loan), it knows that the loan can be sold. Since a large percentage of primary lenders make loans with the intention of selling them, they only make loans that conform to the requirements of the secondary market.

The sale of your loan generally does not affect your interest rate. The secondary lender buys loans based on prevailing interest rates. If a retailer wants to sell the loan, it knows the interest rate that it must charge to sell at face value. If a higher rate is charged, the loan may be sold at a *premium* — an amount higher than face value. If lower than the prevailing rate is charged, the loan will be sold at a *discount*, meaning less than face value.

What the Secondary Market Means to You

Different secondary lenders have different guidelines that must be met before it will buy a loan. For example, Fannie Mae and Freddie Mac have a limit on the loan amount they can purchase for each loan. The limit

changes as real estate prices change, and is different in different regions of the country. Also, many of the participants in the secondary market only buy certain types of loans. To meet these guidelines, many originating lenders specialize in a particular type of mortgage. This helps the primary lender know who will be buying loans it makes and if it will have a problem selling it on the secondary market.

Armed with that knowledge, a smart borrower shops around for a lender that specializes in the type of loan he or she wants. That lender will be more knowledgeable and more efficient in obtaining the loan. Understanding which loan is best for you is the focus of the rest of the book. However, many lenders will simply try to sell you the loan they know best because it is easier for them. If it is not the loan that is best for you, do not stay with that lender.

From the Expert

A lender can make a mortgage loan without following anyone's guidelines, as long as the loan does not violate the law. Any lender keeping the loan for its portfolio follows its own guidelines.

There is a secondary market for all loans—even those made by individuals selling their home and providing the financing to the buyer themselves. It consists of individuals and companies that specialize in buying these mortgages. Without the larger players, this is a much smaller market. Since these mortgages are usually sold at a substantial discount (much less than their face value), it may be more difficult to find a lender providing loans that can be sold in this market. The buyers in this secondary market have their own guidelines, which may be very different from the large institutions like Fannie Mae and Freddie Mac.

Chapter 3

Underwriting

When you apply for a mortgage loan, the success of your application depends on underwriting. *Underwriting* is the process used to decide whether to accept or reject a loan application. It is also used to qualify a borrower for a loan program. When qualifying, it is not an all-or-nothing scenario. A borrower may be rejected for the least expensive loan, but approved for a higher risk, more expensive loan.

There has been a major change in the underwriting process in the past decade. Today, fewer and fewer people do the actual underwriting—instead, it is done by computers. This is called *automated underwriting*. As the name implies, a machine (rather than a person) does the work, and approves or rejects the application. Somewhat surprisingly, this has been a major benefit to many borrowers. It turns out that it was much tougher to get approved by a person than by a machine. The computer has been programmed in most instances to be much more forgiving for problems with credit, income, and debt than were the human underwriters. The computer does not worry about losing its job if it approves too many bad loans.

Regardless of whether a person or computer is actually doing the underwriting, there are three major factors that are considered in the underwriting process: credit, income-to-debt comparison, and property value-to-loan comparison (down payment).

Credit History

The term *credit history* merely refers to how you have managed your credit and debt over a period of years. It looks at how you have financed purchases, as well as how you made your payments on the amounts financed. It is used by lenders to evaluate how you will handle future loans. They look at your past to predict your future.

A bad credit history has become an increasing problem. There are two basic reasons for this. First, it has become very easy to get credit. You are probably inundated every day with solicitations from credit card companies. College students can now easily get credit cards without any work history. Auto dealers advertise that they will sell a car to people with no credit history or a bad credit history. This allows many people to receive credit who cannot handle it. The inevitable result is a failure to pay the debt on time or at all.

The second reason is that these loose lending practices cause many people to believe that paying bills on time is not very important. Much of this comes from advertising. Companies, even some dealing with mortgages, say things like "bad credit shows that you are *only human.*" Since credit is easy to obtain — even with a poor credit history — paying on time does not seem to be very important.

But when it comes time to try to buy a house, a good credit history is a major factor. To some lenders, it is the most important factor. For example, many retirees are able to get loans that their income does not seem to support. This is because they have excellent credit. The lender believes that they will budget properly and repay the loan.

Credit Cards and Credit History

A good way to understand why so many people have a bad credit history is to examine the use of a credit card. There are two ways to use a credit card. One is as a convenience. Those who use credit cards solely for convenience tend to not want to carry a lot of cash and find writing checks to be a nuisance. They pay for their purchases with their credit card and each month pay the bill in full.

If this describes you, you have made the credit card a useful tool. You may even get extra benefits, such as cash back or airline miles. However, in the credit card industry, you are called a *deadbeat*. Using a credit card to your benefit is not what the credit card company had in mind when it issued the card. Some credit card companies will charge you a fee for not making installment payments (paying interest). Even though the credit card company charges a fee to the seller of your purchases, the big money is made on interest paid by the credit card holder. Further, while you have made your credit cards a valuable tool, you are not developing a credit history, as it mainly looks at how you handle making payments, so it can determine how you will handle making a thirty-year mortgage payment.

The second way to use a credit card is to pay less than the total monthly bill, thereby costing you an interest payment. You are borrowing money every time you use your credit card, and what that costs you depends on how you use the card. While paying this interest is certainly costing you money, it is giving you a credit history you can use to later borrow greater sums of money, such as what you will need to buy a house. But all of this depends on your ability to properly manage your credit cards and your payments.

> ### From the Expert
> If you pay in full every month, you are, in effect, never making a monthly payment at all. This saves you money on monthly interest charges to your credit card, but may cost you money in a higher interest rate on a mortgage loan.

How Do You Think of Credit Card Use?

When you see some jewelry or clothing that you would like to own, do you ask yourself if you want it badly enough to borrow money and pay interest to have it? When you go out to eat, do you wonder if you want the meal in that restaurant badly enough to borrow money to eat there? Many, if not most, do not think to ask themselves these questions. This can lead to overspending, and forces many to pay interest on the new clothing or meals for many months to come. While you want some interest

payments to show up, you want to be in control of the cards—not the cards in control of you.

Another common abuse of credit is excessive optimism. Do you really believe that you will never get sick or that your car will never break down? Do you have cash put away for such possibilities? Do you realize that the kids need clothes for school in September or that you may spend more money in December for holiday gifts than you will spend at other times of the year? Have you prepared by saving cash, or will you have to charge everything and make monthly payments?

All of these financial planning failures can get to a point where paying bills on time becomes difficult. When an underwriter looks at your credit history, he or she is looking to see if you borrowed money and repaid it in a timely manner. Did you keep your promise to make payments on time? If so, chances are your promise to repay the loan for which you are applying will be kept. If you did not keep past promises, the underwriter must wonder if you will keep future ones.

What to Do

Before applying for your loan, get a copy of your credit report. You can obtain a copy directly from a credit bureau or a company that will get you one from all the major credit bureaus. You can find these companies in the phone book under "Credit Reporting Agencies," or on the Internet by searching for the same keywords.

You are now entitled to one free credit report from each of the major credit reporting agencies a year. You can get it by calling 877-322-8228 or online at **www.annualcreditreport.com**. If you need to obtain more than your one free report, the cost for additional reports should be under $40; less if you go directly to the credit bureaus. If you have been refused credit based on your credit report, the credit bureau will give you a free report even if you have already gotten your free annual report. You will need the letter showing that you were refused credit. It is wise to get a report from all three bureaus because they may not be the same.

Equifax Credit Information Services, Inc.
P.O. Box 740241
Atlanta, GA 30374
To order report: 800-685-1111
To report fraud: 800-525-6285
www.equifax.com

Experian (formerly TRW)
National Consumer Assistance Center
P.O. Box 2104
Allen, TX 75013
To order report: 888-397-3742
To report fraud: 888-397-3742
www.experian.com

TransUnion LLC
Consumer Disclosure Center
P.O. Box 2000
Chester, PA 19022
To order report: 800-916-8800
To report fraud: 800-680-7289
www.transunion.com

Examine the report for errors. Perhaps the credit bureau mistakenly put information about someone else on your report. Report any errors to the credit bureau. Get something in writing saying that the incorrect information is being removed, and save it. You can at least show the letter to your prospective lender. You may find that it is not easy to get the mistake removed. It may be temporarily removed and then show up again later. Having something in writing will make it easier to get the error removed a second (or repeated) time. After making sure the information from each credit agency is accurate, you can get a good idea of your position as a borrower by checking one figure on each report—your credit score.

Your Credit Score

The importance of the individual underwriter's examination of credit has greatly diminished in recent years. This is due to computer underwriting and the *credit score*. Your credit score is a number determined by a complex mathematical formula. The *Fair Isaacs Corporation* (FICO) invented the credit score and is the dominant company supplying the formula. Your credit score is commonly referred to as your *FICO score*.

Not all lenders use FICO scores, and some do not use them for all the loans that they offer. However, the number of lenders using FICO scores is increasing. It will not be long before almost all lenders will rely on them to some degree in making decisions of approval, rates, and fees.

Lenders use your credit score to both decide whether to accept or reject a mortgage application and to set interest rates and fees. Acceptable scores range from 500 to 850. The interest rate difference can be substantial—over 3%—from low to high. On a $150,000 loan, for example, your monthly payment could be over $300 per month higher if you scored 500 rather than if you scored 850. The average score ranges between 620 and 650.

Lenders advertise interest rates based on the lowest rate they offer. This means that they are assuming that you are the ideal borrower. Do not assume that because a lender advertises a low rate, and also advertises that it will accept borrowers with bad credit, that the low rate applies to the borrower with bad credit.

Unfortunately, an exceptionally high credit score will not get you a rate lower than the bank's best rate. The score needed for the best rate is generally between 720 and 750, depending on the lender. Any score above that will not lower the rate further. However, a great credit score of 800 or above could minimize a problem, such as insufficient income, and still allow you to get a loan someone in the same position with a lower credit score could not.

A benefit of the credit score is that you can determine in advance the approximate interest rate you should pay for your loan. You can even take steps to improve your score—if you plan in advance.

Improving Your Credit Score

The first thing to do to improve your credit score is to get your score from the three major credit companies—Experian, TransUnion, and Equifax—as previously described. Along with giving you your score, they will give you advice on how to raise it. Most of the advice is just using common sense:

- bring debts that are delinquent current;
- be sure to pay bills on time;
- pay off small debts; and,
- cancel unnecessary credit cards.

If you have a low score because you have little or no credit established, you may want to apply for a no-fee credit card or two. While people who pay cash for everything may be the most financially responsible, the credit score formula does not feel the same way. It wants to know how you have handled credit in the past, not how you have avoided using it.

> ### From the Expert
> The idea behind improving your credit score is to make yourself look more financially responsible.

Many lenders want to see the borrower's credit history for at least two years. Mortgage brokers sometimes advise young people with a shorter credit history to ask a parent to add them to a credit card. If the parent has a two- or three-year-old credit card with on-time payments, adding the borrower will show up as part of the borrower's credit history. The practice is unethical, but there have not been any publicized prosecutions for illegally attempting to deceive a lender.

Each positive step you take can raise your score ten to twenty points over a three-month period. Major steps, such as substantially lowering your debt, will result in a higher increase. If you are thinking that you would like to buy a house in a year, now is the time to start working on your credit history. Since you must allow yourself at least three months to change your score (longer to raise your score an appreciable amount), do not wait until you are ready to buy.

Income-to-Debt Ratios

The next thing an underwriter will examine is how much money you earn and how much you owe. From this, ratios are created that become benchmarks for deciding what type of loan you can afford.

The traditional ratios were 25%–35%. This meant that the most your mortgage payment should be was 25% of your gross (total) income. If your salary was $4000 per month, you should pay no more than $1000 per month for your mortgage payment, which included principal, interest, property taxes, and insurance (PITI). This ratio of income to PITI, is called the *top ratio*.

You were then allowed an additional 10% of your income for other debts. Your monthly payments for all debts, including your mortgage, could not exceed 35%. This is called the *bottom ratio*. If your ratios exceeded these numbers, you would have to seek a loan from a high-risk lender and pay higher interest and fees.

The percentage numbers change depending on how badly lenders want to make loans in a given economy. The current trend has lenders raising acceptable numbers. It is not uncommon to get a low-interest loan with numbers like 28% for your mortgage payment and 40% overall. A high credit score will help.

Another variation is a high mortgage ratio and a low overall or total ratio. If you are going to pay 30% of your income for your mortgage expense but have no other debt, you are above one ratio but below the other. Your lender's policy and your credit score will be the determining factors.

In most instances, the policy of the individual lender will determine the ratio. You can simply ask a prospective lender or mortgage broker the numbers they use to give their most favorable interest rate.

Improving Your Ratios

Unless you have a lot of cash on hand, you are going to need time to improve your ratios. Paying down credit cards, instead of paying minimum payments or making additional payments on your car or financed furniture

and appliances is what may be needed. If you know that you are getting a salary increase shortly, time your loan application accordingly.

From the Expert
The added benefit of paying down debt is that it will also improve your credit score.

It is also important to know which debts to pay. Most underwriting, especially automated underwriting, will not consider debts that have less than ten months left to payoff. However, the normal tendency is to pay off debts that have only a few months left. You would benefit more by making an extra payment on a debt with eleven months to go — bringing it down to nine months — than paying a debt off completely with just a few months left.

Finally, sometimes there is another way to exceed the ratios. If you are refinancing your home and have lots of *equity* (equity is the difference between what you owe on your mortgage and the value of your property), a lender may give you a *conditional approval*. The approval may be conditioned on you paying down or paying off some existing debt. You may be able to borrow a little more money on your mortgage loan from your equity and pay down your debts to meet the condition.

Be careful of conditional acceptances. Some lenders are just trying to get you to borrow more money from them. If your debt ratios are good and you are current on your bills, you should question why this is necessary.

Some lenders will also try to get you to borrow more money to *consolidate* your bills. This may have nothing to do with credit or income-to-debt ratios. You will be given monthly payment numbers showing that you can lower your interest rates and monthly payments by using additional borrowing on the mortgage to pay off your car, credit cards, etc.

It is true that you will save money initially. However, you will effectively have, for example, a fifteen- to thirty-year car payment, depending on the length of your mortgage. It takes great discipline to take that savings every month and put it away to buy a new car. Are you going to now pay cash for your purchases or just run up the credit card debt again? Many people find that within a short time, they have the same debt they

had before they consolidated, in addition to a bigger monthly mortgage payment. Unless you are extremely disciplined or extremely desperate, stay away from consolidation loans.

The Property

The final consideration in seeking a loan is the real estate involved. The standards have changed in the last few years because of low interest rates, the rising cost of real estate, and the availability of money to lend. However, there are still two things to consider—the loan-to-value ratio and the down payment.

Loan-to-Value Ratios

One of the standard procedures before making a loan is to determine the value of the property. This is done by an appraisal, which determines a value for the property for the loan purposes. The lender may have its own appraisers (in-house appraisers) or they may use an independent (outside) appraiser.

There are several different types of appraisals, some of which are highly complicated and require special education and licensing. Appraising a home, especially a tract house or condominium, is relatively easy. The most common appraisal method used is to compare similar properties that have recently sold. A computer database with this information is available to the appraiser, who physically inspects the subject property to assess its condition. It is then valued based on the sale prices of similar properties in the area, called comparables or *comps*. If the comps are not exactly the same model as the subject property, a price adjustment is made for square footage, lot size, and any amenities, such as a swimming pool or room addition.

For certain types of loans in which there is an extremely low loan-to-value ratio, the lender may even use a *desktop* appraisal. With this method, the values of comparable properties are checked on a computer and there is no physical examination of the property beyond a *drive by*.

The amount of money you ask the bank to lend you compared to the value of the property is the loan-to-value ratio. The lower the ratio, the lower the risk for the lender. For you, the lower the ratio, the lower your credit score can be.

Example: If you wanted to borrow 50% of the value of the property, your credit score would not need to be as high as if you wanted to borrow 90%.

NOTE: *As you have probably noticed by now, your credit score keeps coming up in all phases of the loan. A high credit score will not just give you a better chance to get a loan — it will also save you money on certain fees and on interest.*

Down Payments

The appraisal serves another purpose — it can have a significant impact on the amount of the down payment. In a *seller's market*, when buyers are many and sellers are few, property may be overpriced. You are free, of course, to pay any amount you wish for the property you buy. The problem arises with the loan you can get. For example, if the property you want to buy is appraised at $5000 less than the price you have agreed to pay, your lender will want you to come up with a down payment. That down payment, in addition to meeting the lenders percentage requirement, must make up the $5000 difference.

Traditionally, a conventional (not government-insured or guaranteed) loan required a minimum 20% down payment. Government-insured or guaranteed loans required between 10% to 0% down, depending on the type of loan. Unfortunately, because of the changing standards involving real estate, fewer people have the 20% required down payment. However, there are ways to pay a smaller down payment.

Private Mortgage Insurance

Lenders want to make loans at the lowest risk possible. With a 20% down payment, most lenders are comfortable with the risk level of the loan. To cover risks with down payments of less than 20%, private mortgage

insurance developed. *Private mortgage insurance* (PMI) insures the lender in the event that the foreclosure of a mortgage results in a sale that nets less than the balance owed. The cost of the insurance is paid by the borrower. For a loan with a down payment less than 20% you will have, as part of your monthly mortgage payment, an additional payment for *PMI.*

The insurance does not cover the entire loan amount—only a small percentage. So if you have only 10% to put down, the lender requires you to buy PMI to cover the other 10%. If the lender takes a loss, the insurer will cover that loss up to 10% of the amount of the loan.

> ### From the Expert
> As a general breakdown on what the cost of PMI will be, you can expect to pay between .75% to 1.5% of the loan amount for PMI.

Theoretically, the lender's risk is the same as if it made an 80% loan. As a practical matter, the lender's risk is greater, since 10% down borrowers are more likely to default than 20% down borrowers. The more you put down, the better chance you will get the most favorable interest rate for a loan and have to pay less in PMI.

The rates you will pay for PMI vary, based on the percent covered and the borrower's credit score. Borrowers who put down 5% pay more than those who put down 15%. This makes sense because more insurance is required. It also makes sense that a higher down payment means a lower risk of default.

The lender may have a choice of how much insurance they require. The lender may buy insurance to cover 30% of the loan, rather than 20%. This will cost more. If you are getting PMI, ask if the lender is getting the minimum insurance. If you have good credit and good income-to-debt ratios, you should question why the extra insurance is necessary.

At the time you apply for the loan, you also want to ask about *cancellation* of the PMI. Once you have paid on the loan to a point that PMI should no longer be required, you should stop paying for it or get a refund if you paid the total up front. Laws now require a lender to cancel PMI when the loan-to-value ratio reaches 78% of the value of the property at the time when the loan was made (if cancellation is not requested by

the borrower), and at 80% if the borrower makes a request. Ask about cancellation before taking a loan and always contact your lender when the loan-to-value ratio reaches 80% to have it cancelled.

Many people hate having to pay PMI. There are ways to avoid PMI using different types of loans that will be discussed later. One way to increase your down payment and lower or eliminate PMI is through a gift.

Gifts

Check with your lender to see if all or part of the down payment can be covered by a gift. If you have a relative who is willing to help you with the down payment, get a *gift letter* from that relative (along with the gift) stating that you do not have to pay back the money. How much of your own money you will need depends on the type of loan you are seeking and the lender's policy (which usually contains a minimum credit score requirement).

If you are using a gift as part of your down payment, ask the lender for the form gift letter they want you to use. There is no standard form used by all lenders.

A gift letter must contain:
- The names of the donor (giver of the gift) and the donee (receiver of the gift).
- Whether the gift has been given or only promised. The lender may require that it be given before accepting the letter.
- The purpose of the gift (to help purchase the home). The property address is given in this section.
- A statement that no repayment is required or expected, either in cash or future services. (Although by definition a gift does not have to be repaid, lenders want it emphasized.)
- The relationship of the donor to donee, such as parent or sibling. The donor may also be a nonprofit organization that helps low income buyers or those having a specific job.
- The date and signature of the donor and an acceptance and signature of the donee. Notarizing the signatures is usually not required. If it is, your lender will most likely have a form for you to use.

The lender may also require that the donor disclose the source of the funds, such as the sale of stock, savings account, etc. There may also be a statement that no party to the sale, such as the seller or real estate agent, is the real source of the gift.

If the lender does not provide a form, use the one on page 25. Ask the lender to approve it before you get it signed.

Most lenders want you to have at least 5% of your own money in the deal. You will have to show proof that the money is yours, and not borrowed or a gift. Bank statements showing regular deposits to a savings account, or a letter from your employer stating that you were paid a bonus, are examples of what you may need to show your lender.

Gifts From Strangers

A fast growing availability of gifts is emerging. Local governments and charities are helping those who cannot afford to buy a home because they lack a down payment. These programs are not just for low-income borrowers. There are special programs available in some areas for police officers, firefighters, teachers, and others. Many local governments have decided that people with these jobs benefit the community and have made money available to them to buy homes.

You can review down payment gifts by typing "down payment" into any search engine. If you do not have a computer, your local library generally has one for public use. Before agreeing to anything, check with your realtor, lender, and local government for gifts that you may be qualified to receive. These programs are often local in nature or specific to certain members of the community, so you need to check in your own area. Beware of companies that advertise that they will find a gift for you, as they may charge you to find the gift that you could easily find yourself.

GIFT LETTER

The following letter contains the general requirements for a gift letter. It may contain more than you need. Remember to ask your lender for their specific requirements for your gift letter.

Name(s) of donor(s) _____

Name(s) of donee(s), herein called recipient(s) _____

Relationship of donor(s) to recipient(s) _____

I/We, the above named donor(s) (have given/will give) to the above named recipient(s) the sum of $_____.

This gift is to be used for the purchase of the property located at:

Street address_____

City_____ State_____ Zip Code_____

No repayment is required, expected or implied, either in the form of cash or future services.

Source of funds:

Bank _____ Branch address _____

Account number _____

Other source (explain) _____

_____

No portion of this gift has been given by anyone who is a party to or associated with the sale of the above described property.

Recipient(s) accept(s) this gift as evidenced by the signature(s) below.

Executed this _____ day of _____, 20___

_____   _____
Name of Donor   Name of Recipient

_____   _____
Name of Donor   Name of Recipient

Address of Donor:

Street_____

City_____ State_____ Zip Code_____

Telephone: Area code (   ) Number _____

Chapter 4

Interest Rates

Most people believe that the most expensive purchase they will make is buying a home. They make offers below the asking price, trying to save a few thousand dollars. If a low offer is accepted, they are elated. Then, many of them secure a mortgage loan that costs them tens of thousands of dollars more than they should be paying.

> **Example:** A 30-year loan will almost always cost more than the property. If you buy a home for $100,000 and get a 7% loan for thirty years for $100,000, the total interest on the loan would be $139,508 — making the loan cost you a total of $239,508. The same loan at 6% would have total interest of $115,838.
>
> Suppose you paid 7%, but took the loan for fifteen years. The total interest would be $61,789.40, which is substantially less than the purchase price and less than half what you would pay for the 30-year loan. The 15-year loan at 6% would cost you $51,894.80 in interest.

You can easily see that negotiating the right loan may be more important than negotiating the purchase price of the home. It would be impossible to buy a home listed at $100,000 for $12,386.80. It is possible to save the $87,618.20 on your mortgage buy getting a 6%, 15-year loan instead of a 7%, 30-year loan. If you are going to borrow $200,000 or $300,000, the savings are even more dramatic.

Understanding Interest Rates

When you use someone else's property, you pay for its use. This is called *rent*. People rent everything from apartments to cars to carpet cleaners. The longer you use whatever you are renting, the more you have to pay.

When you want to buy a house and do not want to, or do not have enough money to pay cash, you have to rent the needed money. The rent you pay for the use of this money is called *interest*.

Interest rates are determined by some factors over which you have no control, as well as some that you can control. The rates set by the Federal Reserve that affect mortgage interest rates, for example, are beyond your control. Factors you can control that influence interest rates include the type of loan (fixed-rate, adjustable, or hybrid), term (length) of the loan, your credit score, down payment, and loan-to-value ratio. You can also take some steps to lower your interest rate.

Points and Buydowns

A *point* is simply one percent of the loan amount. It is usually paid in a lump sum when you get your loan. It may be financed in some cases.

There are two types of points. The first is a *discount point,* which can directly lower your interest rate. This is the one you may want.

> **Example:** You want to borrow $150,000. One lender offers a *no points loan* with an interest rate of 6%. Another lender offers a *two points loan* at 5.5%. By paying the two points you are *buying down* the interest rate. Which loan is better?
>
> There are two things you must consider to determine the answer. One is easy, and the other is usually not easy. First type "mortgage points" into any search engine. There will be several sites for mortgage calculators. For the above example, the monthly payment on a 30-year loan would be just under $50 less per month on the two point 5.5% loan. It would take a little over five years to make the two points loan the better deal. Type in your specific numbers and you will be able to figure out the break-even time for the loan amount and percentages you are comparing.

Now for the harder part. How long will it be before you pay off the loan? Are you planning to move within five years (before the break-even time)? If you plan to move in three years, you would want the no points, 6% loan. If you end up staying in the property seven years, you would have saved money with the two points, 5.5% loan. While predicting when you will move in the future is no easy task, most people underestimate the time they will keep their property.

An advantage to discount points is that they are considered interest and are currently tax deductible. Since tax laws change frequently, always get advice or research current deductions for mortgage expenses before filing.

A buydown over the life of a 15- to 30-year loan will not cause a significant difference in your interest rate. The estimate on a 30-year loan, for example, is ⅛ of 1%.

The buydown is most effective over a short period. If you buy down your interest rate for the first three to five years of your loan, the rate and monthly payment will drop enough that it may mean the difference between qualifying and being rejected.

Since the lender will give more weight to you lowering your monthly payment than to having some cash in the bank, you can accomplish more by using available cash to buy down the rate.

The second type of point is the *origination* or *commission point*. These are lender fees or mortgage broker commissions. They do not lower your interest rate or any other costs of the loan. They are a necessary payment for the service that you receive. However, avoiding these fees may not save you money. Paying a fair commission to an honest and competent mortgage broker may be insignificant compared to the money he or she will save you on your mortgage loan.

> **From the Expert**
>
> Since the lender will give more weight to lowering your monthly payment than having some cash in the bank, you can accomplish more by using available cash to buy down the rate.

Back Points

Back points or *yield spread premiums,* as they are more formally called, are commission points paid to the loan originator that are hidden from the borrower. You have heard ads that say that if you refinance your current loan, your payment will decrease, your loan amount will not increase, and not a penny will come out of your pocket. Common sense tells you that the company offering the loan has to be making money somehow.

> **Example:** Assume that you have a current interest rate of 8%. Your payment on a 30-year loan is $1,467.53. Also assume that the best current interest rate you could get is 6%. The company offering the loan is simply a mortgage broker, placing the loan with a lender for a fee. If the lender can get a high enough interest rate, the lender is willing to pay the fee. If you get a loan at 6.5%, the lender is getting a .5% premium. On a $200,000 loan, this approximately costs an extra $1000 per year. The lender is willing to pay the broker offering you the loan a point (1%) for placing the loan. The broker gets $2000, and you get a monthly payment of $1,264.14, with no money out of pocket.

Because the lender is subsidizing your payment of the point, the loan may contain a clause saying that if you pay it off before a certain time, you will have to pay a penalty. This will give the lender back the subsidy if you do not pay on the higher rate long enough to make up the back point paid on your behalf.

If you are using a mortgage broker for a loan with no points, ask what the broker will receive from the lender and how it will affect your loan. If the loan has no points or fees, and the broker says that there are no back points, find a more truthful broker. You know the broker has to be paid by someone. Some questions to ask the broker include the following.

- What is the difference in the interest rate between the no points loan and a loan with one or two points?
- How long must you pay on the loan with points before you break even?

- Is there a prepayment penalty on the no points loan, and if so, what is the amount or formula used to determine the amount?

Locking In Your Loan Rate

Any rate quoted to you by a lender or mortgage broker is subject to change. Even when there are no major trends of rates increasing or decreasing, rates change daily. Since even an eighth of a percent can mean a difference of thousands of dollars over the life of a loan, it is important at some point to have the lender commit to a definite interest rate. This is called *locking in the rate*. There will be a fee charged to lock in the rate, which will vary depending on the duration of the lock. Locking in your rate for sixty days will cost more than for thirty days.

When rates are falling, lenders will offer a low-cost lock-in fee or even lock in your rate free. Some will offer a *float down*. This means that if the rate falls after you lock in, you can get the lower rate. Common practice is that if rates fall after you lock in, you pay the higher rate. Lenders say they are taking the risk that rates will rise, so the borrower should take the risk that rates will fall.

The liberal policies, like no-fee locks and float downs, are usually for adjustable rate loans only. The lock only applies to the start rate, which will last no more than a year (more likely three to six months). The rate then adjusts as agreed in your loan documents, regardless of your lock-in rate. The lock on a fixed-rate loan can set the interest rate for as long as thirty years.

Lenders' lock-in policies vary, and you should be clear that you understand the policies of the different lenders that you are considering. Ask for the information on rate locks in writing. The policies are not simply in the mind of your loan representative. They are written somewhere and should be available to you.

From the Expert

A lender will have a policy less favorable to the borrower on a fixed-rate loan compared to an adjustable loan, since the rate will not change over the entire loan period.

If you know your lender's policy regarding locking in your rate, you have one more bit of knowledge to help you decide which lender to use. The lender with a less favorable lock-in policy may still offer the best overall program. You will not know this unless you know all aspects of the cost of loans, including lock-in costs.

When rates are rising, lenders charge more for locking in the rate and sometimes a disproportionate amount for a long lock-in. It is important that you compare the costs of the lock-in periods and weigh them against the chances of rates increasing that quickly. If rates are relatively stable, you can usually save money by locking in closer to closing time, such as thirty rather than sixty days. A good loan representative or mortgage broker can keep track of rate changes daily. If there is a little dip, he or she can alert you to lock in. You can follow mortgage interest rates yourself in financial newspapers, financial sections of some major newspapers, or on the Internet. Type "mortgage rates" into a search engine and take your pick.

Assumable Mortgages and Prepayment Penalties

When talking about interest rates, there are a couple of other things you should know. Clauses can be inserted into mortgages that really only have impact in times when it is anticipated that interest rates will be changing. Often, these clauses are not inserted at all, but depend on your anticipated circumstance and market conditions when you want to sell you home (or, in some cases, buy a home).

An *assumable loan* is one that can be taken over by a buyer of the mortgaged property. In a market where interest rates are going up, it can be a major factor in a sale.

Example: You have a mortgage against your property with an interest rate of 6%. When you decide to sell your home, interest rates are 8%. If a buyer can assume your 6% loan instead of getting a new loan at 8%, your property becomes more desirable. You may even be able to get a higher price and still save the buyer some money.

Lenders are, of course, aware of the loss they will take if a buyer assumes the low interest loan rather than getting a new, higher interest loan. To prevent this, they rarely offer a fixed-rate loan that is assumable. They instead restrict assumable loans to those mortgages that call for the interest rate to adjust to market rates.

The *prepayment penalty* is opposite of the assumable loan, in that it is used most effectively in a falling interest rate market. If your mortgage is 8% and rates when you decide to sell are 6%, your buyer is not going to want to assume your loan. Lenders know that having 8% loans replaced by 6% loans is not as profitable as continuing the 8% loans and so charge a prepayment penalty.

Simply put, a prepayment penalty means that if you pay off or pay down your loan too soon, you pay a penalty. Since there is generally a surge of refinancing as interest rates fall, the lender makes up some of the loss that is incurred by replacing high-interest loans with lower interest loans.

There is no standard prepayment penalty for all loans. The most common prepayment penalty clauses are reviewed with the specific loans discussed in later chapters. When you apply for a loan, always ask if there is a prepayment penalty.

Chapter 5

Prequalifying for a Loan

Before you start looking at homes, you should know how much you can borrow. There are several ways to determine this amount.

In order to prequalify, you need to gather some information—including your credit report, your income-to-debt ratios, and the amount of your down payment. You should also have some cash for points and fees.

Using a Real Estate Agent

A good real estate agent will ask you to fill out a simple form to determine your debt ratios and get your credit score (if you do not already have it). This is simply good business, since no agent wants to waste time showing you homes that you have no chance to buy.

However, the agent will most likely show you the highest priced homes for which you can qualify. This is also good business, since you are more likely to fall in love with a higher priced home than a less expensive one. Once you fall in love, it is an easy sale. Remember, once you look at the most you can possibly afford, less expensive homes will be disappointing. Always try to look at the least expensive homes first and work your way up until you find one that satisfies both your needs and desires.

Using the Web

If you want to avoid seeing the most expensive homes first or you want to check out homes for sale by the owner with no agent, prequalify your-

self for a mortgage. To do this, type "mortgage calculators" into any search engine. Look at several to get an idea of how they work. You want to find one that allows you to figure out how much you can borrow without someone calling to sell you a loan. If you are asked to give personal information, go to another website.

One website that has good information without requiring any identifying information from you is **www.mortgage-calc.com**.

When you find one you like, type in several interest rates to see the payment differences. Since you do not know yet exactly what your rate will be, this will help you come up with a range of affordable prices. Also, see if you can possibly afford a less than 30-year loan.

Some of the calculators even compare costs of buying and renting. If you have never owned a home, this could be helpful. Many people simply compare the mortgage payment with their rent. There are many other expenses to home ownership, such as taxes, insurance, and maintenance.

Using a Lender

Another way to prequalify is to go to a lender (a bank, for example) and ask to be prequalified. A prequalified acceptance by a lender is a good indicator, but is not a guarantee, that you will be accepted for a certain loan amount. Always make your offer to purchase contingent upon getting your loan. If you do not, you become a cash buyer.

> **From the Expert**
>
> You can lose your deposit if you cannot complete the purchase and do not protect yourself with the contingency.

There is a difference between prequalifying and being preapproved. When you *prequalify*, the lender simply takes your word for the information you supply. When you are *preapproved*, the lender has verified this information.

Even preapproval is not a guarantee of final loan acceptance, because interest rates may change. Higher rates mean higher payments, and that could mean you no longer qualify for the same loan amount. Only when the lender commits to an interest rate (locks in the rate) can you be sure that you qualify.

Once you have determined how much you can most likely borrow, a good strategy is to cut that amount by ten percent. If you calculate that you can qualify for a monthly payment of $1000, use $900 as your goal. This will serve two purposes. First, it will give you a little cushion if interest rates turn out to be a little higher than you anticipated. Second, you will not stretch yourself so thin that even a small, unexpected expense will cause financial difficulty.

Tell your real estate agent that you do not want to pay more than $900 per month for a fixed-rate, fully amortized loan. This will be the highest payment type of loan. If you like a home that you see for that payment, you are making a sensible purchase. If you absolutely hate the homes in that payment range, you can raise your sights a little. You may still keep the $900 a month payment (at least for a while) by getting an adjustable or hybrid loan. (These are discussed in a later chapter.)

Once you know how much you can prequalify for, do not start shopping for a home before you understand some of the additional components common to the mortgages, the different types of loans available, and their variations. You can then calculate qualifying for the type of loan that is best for your situation.

Chapter 6

The Term

Since a mortgage is usually the largest purchase you will ever make, how long it takes to pay it off should be a major concern. The *term* is the number of years that it will take to pay off the loan if all required payments are made on time and there are no extra payments made. Selecting the proper term can save you more money than any other feature of a loan.

Although an increasing number of lenders are offering 10- and 20-year mortgages, the most common choice from most lenders is between a 15-year loan and a 30-year loan. If you are dealing with a lender offering 10- or 20-year mortgages, the following considerations apply equally to these terms.

Assuming that you can qualify for shorter than a 30-year term, there are several factors to consider when deciding whether a shorter or longer term is right for you. The most important is whether you are confident that you can make the higher payment required on the 15-year loan. Ask your lender what the payments would be on each for the amount that you intend to borrow. If you do not have a lender yet, use one of the online calculators to compute the difference.

Examine your spending habits, as well as your current and future budgeting. For example, if you are not currently making car payments, but plan to buy a new car with payments, you have to add the probable car payments to your future expenses. If you eat out three times a week in a good restaurant, there could be a saving of two or three hundred dollars a month if you cut back to once or twice a week.

Once you feel comfortable that you could make the larger payment on the 15-year loan, go to the next step. What will you do with the money

you *save* by making the lower payment on the 30-year loan?

If you have a specific reason for wanting the lower payment (beyond the financial need for it), such as investing the money, you have to compare the return on the investment to the return on the 15-year loan compared to the 30-year loan. This is something that your financial planner will have to advise you on, taking into consideration your specific circumstances and goals.

If you do not have any special reason for wanting the lower payment, the 15-year loan has several advantages. The major advantage to the 15-year loan is that the interest rate, as well as the fees, will be lower than the 30-year loan. When you combine this with the higher payments because of the shorter term, the results are dramatic.

> **Example:** On a $100,000 loan at 7%, you would pay slightly under $6000 in principal during the first five years. By paying only .25% less for your 15-year loan (a fairly standard offering), you would pay just under $23,000 in principal during the same five years. The payment on the 15-year loan would be $220 per month higher. By paying $13,200 ($220 x 60 months) you reduce your loan by an additional $17,000, and you only have ten years to go (as opposed to twenty-five).

If you are in your 40s or older, it makes sense to have a free and clear home before retirement. Chapter 22 on reverse mortgages shows just how important this can be.

If you do not feel comfortable with the higher payment, all is not lost. You can get the 30-year loan and make additional principal payments. You will not save as much because of the higher interest rate, but you can still substantially reduce the loan term. It will take more discipline since the additional payments on the 30-year loan are voluntary, while the higher payment on the 15-year loan is required.

Chapter 7

Payment Plans

Before you can make any meaningful comparison of types of loans available, you must compare monthly payments. There are loans where the monthly payment is the primary feature of the loan. When you apply for one of these loans, you are looking at the monthly payment as the reason for taking this loan over a loan with similar or the same interest rate, term, etc.

Without taking into consideration additions to your monthly payment amount, such as for PMI and funds in escrow for taxes and insurance, your monthly payment is made up of two components—principal and interest. *Principal* is the amount of money that you borrowed or owe on the loan at any given time. *Interest* is most easily understood as the rent you are paying for the use of the principal. As you pay down the principal amount, you pay less rent (interest).

In a standard loan, called an *interest included, level payment loan*, your payment is the same each month. However, how the money is allocated changes.

Example: If your loan is for $100,000 and your payment is $1000 per month, very little of your first payment will go toward principal. This is because you are paying interest on $100,000 dollars.

If, of your $1000 payment, $100 goes toward principal reduction and $900 is interest, you will have a slightly higher amount going toward principal reduction and less to interest on your next payment. This is because your first payment reduced your principal

balance (the amount you owe) by $100. With your second payment, you are paying interest on $99,900 instead of $100,000.

As you keep making payments and reducing the principal amount, the allocation of the monthly payment will continue to change. When you reduce your principal balance in half, for example, more of your payment will be going to principal than to interest. When you get close to paying off your loan, almost all of your payment will go to principal.

Other payment plans exist that differ from the standard plan and can be of benefit to some borrowers. One plan, which concerns only the payment aspect of the loan, can be used with any type of principal reduction loan. This is the *biweekly payment plan*. A second is a specific type of loan that has payment amounts as its main feature. It is the *graduated payment mortgage*. The third is the *interest-only mortgage*, which features the lowest possible payment over the life of the loan. The final one is a cross between interest only and full amortization. This is the *balloon payment mortgage*.

Biweekly Payment Plans

The *biweekly payment plan* is another way to reduce the total interest that you will pay over the life of your loan (and, consequently, reduce the term).

The purpose of the plan is money management. If your payday is every other week, you make your payment before you have a chance to spend the money on other things. For many borrowers, paying extra on payday is easier than putting that money aside to make an additional principal payment once a month.

From the Expert

For those with little financial discipline, a biweekly payment plan is easier than paying the required monthly payment.

The plan sounds simple. You pay half your monthly payment every two weeks. Since there are more than twenty-eight days in all months except February, you are paying a little extra. If your payment is $1000 per month, for example, you would make the required payment of $12,000 per year. If you paid

half the monthly payment every two weeks, you would pay $500 times 26, for a total of $13,000 per year.

The results are surprising. On a $100,000 loan for thirty years at 7% interest, you will save over $34,000 in interest over the life of the loan and pay it off over six years sooner (approximately six years and four months sooner). Sounds good so far.

The problems are in the mechanics of applying the extra money. There are three common ways that lenders apply the extra money paid.

1. The extra money is credited to principal every two weeks. This is the *true* biweekly payment plan and will give the results described above.

2. The extra money is held in an account and credited to principal once a month. This is the *standard* (sometimes called *pseudo*) plan. Over the life of the loan described above, the standard plan will cost the borrower about $2000 and increase the term by four months over the true plan.

3. The third method is to hold the money in an account and apply it to principal once a year. This will be even less advantageous to the borrower. If this is the plan offered, find another lender.

Biweekly plans should be arranged directly with the lender. If you are getting a new loan, this is a simple matter. Ask if the lender offers a biweekly plan and how the extra money is applied. Most lenders do not offer such a payment plan. It is simply not to their advantage.

If your lender does not accept biweekly payments or you already have an existing mortgage, it is more difficult. Few lenders offer a way to switch over to a true biweekly plan. The best option you are likely to get will be that you can send in half your monthly payment every two weeks and the extra money will be applied once a month.

Beware of companies that offer to change you to a biweekly plan. If your lender will not do it for you, it will not do it for them. What these companies do is collect the biweekly payment from you and send it to your lender monthly as an additional principal payment. Some even keep the extra money and make the additional payment once a year. On top of

drawing interest on your money while they are holding it, they charge a fee for their service.

A better way is to do it yourself. Arrange with your lender to have your payment taken directly from your bank account. Deposit half your monthly payment into the account every two weeks. At the end of each month, send the extra money to the lender as an additional principal payment. You can ask the lender to automatically withdraw the extra money from your account each month, but they probably will not agree to do it.

The difference, of course, between doing it yourself and having a company do it for you is discipline. If you get a bill every two weeks from the company handling the payment for you, you will pay it. If you do not have to put that extra money into your account, it will take more discipline to do it. If you had that little financial discipline, you would not be looking into buying a home and getting the best loan.

Discussing fixed-rate versus adjustable rate loans in a general way is easy. It becomes more difficult when you get down to specifics. You will have many choices of both fixed and adjustable rate loans, as you will see in following chapters.

> ### From the Expert
> If you intend to pay on your loan for ten years or more, a fixed rate, biweekly payment mortgage is definitely the best loan you can get. If you intend to sell within ten years, there is less of an advantage. If you intend to sell within five years, an adjustable rate loan will usually be better for you.

Graduated Payment Mortgage

The *graduated payment mortgage* is particularly beneficial to the young borrower. This type of loan was designed to help a borrower whose income was expected to increase after the purchase.

Before examining graduated payment mortgages, we should define the term *amortization*. The word *amortize* comes from the French word *mort*, meaning *dead*. When you amortize (pay off) a loan, you kill it (make it dead). The phrase *life of the loan* is used as a synonym for term of the loan. The word *amortize* has come to mean paying down the principal as

well as paying in full. If you are told that your loan will be amortized over thirty years, it means that if you make the required payment, you will pay the loan in full in thirty years.

The graduated payment mortgage starts off with a very low payment. The payment is lower than even the interest portion of the loan payment amount. This means that the amount you owe on your loan will actually increase, even though you are making your required payments. This is called *negative amortization*.

Each year, the amount you pay will increase to make up for the negative amortization. There are different rates of increase depending on your specific loan agreement, but a common increase is 7.5% per year for five years. At the end of five years, your payment will stay the same for the rest of the term. This stable payment will be higher than if you originally got a fixed-rate loan.

The risk is obvious. You are counting on being in a better financial situation in the future so that you are able to make the increasing payment amounts. In the past, a better future financial position was taken as a given. For example, union contracts were always renewed with wage and benefit increases. In those cases, this type of loan carried little risk for a union member. Today, jobs are less secure and pay raises are even less secure. Look at unions whose members work for airlines, and the risk is obvious.

The benefit with the graduated payment mortgage is that it may be easier to qualify for. Since the mortgage expense part of qualifying is based on your initial monthly payment, you can see the advantage. Your initial monthly payment is even lower than an interest-only loan. (See the next section for details.) However, this is a high-risk loan. You should be fairly certain that you will be able to meet the future increased payments.

There is some relief to the risks associated with this loan. If you believe that you live in an area with rising housing prices, you may have some built-in protecction. If you cannot afford the increased payment amount, you will be able to sell your property and have some money to relocate to something you can afford. Of course, if housing prices are rising, it will be more expensive for you to stay in the same area.

Interest-Only Loans

The interest-only payment loan is often used when housing prices are high. By paying only the interest, you get the benefit of a lower monthly payment. This will not only make the payment easier to manage, but it will allow you to qualify for a higher loan. This allows you to buy a higher priced property.

The obvious drawback is that you never reduce the amount that you owe. At some point in time you will have to pay off your loan. You will still owe all that you originally borrowed.

Interest-only loans can be for a shorter term than loans that require payments to include a reduction of the principal. You can get an interest-only loan for as little as five years, sometimes even less. Most other types of first mortgages have a minimum ten-year term, but are typically set at fifteen.

If housing prices are rising, interest-only loans can be very beneficial. You can buy a higher priced property and still have a payment that you can handle. You can then refinance as the value of your property increases.

Another advantageous situation is if you buy a *fixer upper*. If you buy a property in poor condition and renovate it, you will certainly increase its value. This should enable you to refinance when the renovation is completed. You will also have more money to make the repairs, since your interest-only mortgage will have a low monthly payment.

There are risks. If the value of your property does not increase, you will not be able to refinance. You will not be able to sell your property if prices fall below what you owe. Unless you can come up with the money to pay off the loan, you will lose your home. Again, you will be in a bad situation.

The second risk is if you would not have qualified unless you got the interest-only loan. If your income and debt situation does not change before the balloon payment is required, you still will not be able to qualify for a standard loan or other principal reduction loan. This risk is not as great as long as property values do not fall, since you will probably be

able to get another interest-only loan. However, the risk must be considered.

Paying interest only has two equally unpleasant consequences. The first is that you never build equity by paying down the amount you originally borrowed. If you borrow $100,000, for example, and pay interest only for thirty years, you will still owe $100,000.

> ## __From the Expert__
> With the interest-only loan, you never reduce the principal. Your interest amount is always based on the amount that you originally borrowed.

The second consequence is that you pay more interest. With any loan, your interest is based on your principal balance. With a principal reduction loan, your principal balance becomes less each time you make a payment. This reduces the amount of interest on the subsequent payment. As you near the end of your loan term, almost all of your payment is going toward principal reduction and very little is going toward interest.

For most people, the advantage of a principal reduction loan over the interest-only loan is the forced saving feature. With a loan that requires a payment that reduces your principal balance, you are forced to build equity in your home. Because you reduce the principal with each payment, more of each future payment goes to paying the principal. With an interest-only loan, you reduce the principal only if you pay more than the required amount.

There is one clear advantage to the interest-only loan. Since your payment is based on your loan balance, any additional payment above interest only will reduce your monthly payment. With the principal reduction loan your payment stays the same, regardless of your balance.

Example: You borrow $100,000 at 6% interest for thirty years. Your monthly payment on a standard fixed-rate, fully amortized loan (principal reduction loan) is $599.55 (round to $600). Every payment for thirty years will be $600.

The same terms on an interest-only loan would require a payment of $500 (6% of $100,000 divided by 12). If you paid $100 extra each month, you would reduce your loan at the end of one year by

$1200, to make it $98,800. Your payment (interest only) would now be 6% of $98,800, divided by 12, which is $494.

If you paid an extra $1200 during the second year, you would reduce your payment even more since you'd be paying an extra $106 per month toward principal reduction.

NOTE: *These calculations are not exact. Since you are paying the additional $100 monthly, you reduce your required payment monthly. This gives you a slightly lower required payment each month. Using approximate numbers gives you the idea of how it works without a complicated table.*

By paying extra on the interest-only loan, you have reduced your monthly payment as well as built equity. Even if you continue to pay the extra $100 per month, you will be paying less than the $600 per month you would have to pay on the principal reduction loan.

Interest Extra Loans

A variation of the interest-only loan is the *interest extra loan*. This variation can act as a principal reduction loan while reducing your payment. With an interest extra loan, you pay a fixed amount each month on the principal.

Example: You have $100,000 loan, with your first payment of $1000 allocated $900 to interest and $100 to principal. Since you reduced your principal by $100, you now owe $99,900. Your second payment would be $100 toward principal and slightly less than $900 in interest, since you now owe $99,900 instead of $100,000. The payment would continue to fall, since each monthly payment would be based on what you owe, not what you originally borrowed.

The loan works best if you pay a large amount per month toward the principal. Since you are reducing your principal amount quickly, you are correspondingly reducing your interest quickly—and thus, your total payment quickly.

This type of loan is ideal for borrowers with good present income that is expected to fall. A working couple that expects one or both to retire in ten years would be good candidates. By the time they face lower income, their mortgage payment would be substantially lower. They would not have to refinance in order to lower the payment. Unfortunately, this type of loan is not offered by your average lender.

This loan is simply a variation of the commonly used interest-only loan. The difference is that with an interest-only loan, the borrower can only reduce the principal by voluntary payments in excess of the required payment. The interest extra loan requires a payment higher than interest only, forcing the borrower to reduce the principal.

Balloon Payment Mortgages

A *balloon payment* is a lump-sum payment at the end of the term of a loan, when the monthly payments over the term are not sufficient to amortize (pay off) the loan. For example, at the end of an interest-only loan, the remaining balance must be made with a lump sum, ballon payment.

There are variations that fall between interest-only and full amortization loans. These are loans that base the payment on a term different from the actual term. A typical one is a 30/5 loan. This means that the payment is based on thirty years, but the loan must be repaid in five years. The required payments are not enough to pay off the loan, creating the balloon payment at the end of the five-year term.

The obvious question is what happens at the end of the five-year term? You can, of course, pay the balloon by refinancing. You are betting that rates will not rise too much in that five-year period.

You can also sell the property. If your plan in getting this loan is that you intend to sell before the balloon is due, that is a good reason. The interest rate may be lower on the balloon mortgage compared to an adjustable rate mortgage.

Today's balloon mortgages will usually have a refinance clause. They will typically guarantee that the lender will either extend the term of the existing loan (modify it) or give the borrower a new loan. There are usu-

ally some fees involved in the modification and always in the refinance. In addition, there are generally two requirements.

First, the borrower must not be delinquent on the payments. This just makes sense — if you cannot pay your existing loan, why would the lender want to extend it or give you a new loan?

Second, is the interest rate. You are going to get the extension or new loan at the prevailing rates five years after the original loan. You can see the problem if rates rise dramatically. Unless the lender will guarantee a limit on the interest rate for the modification or refinance, you are at the mercy of the market.

An alternative is an adjustable rate mortgage with a low interest rate for the first five years. (see Chapter 9.) It will probably cost you more than the balloon mortgage, but it will have a limit on the amount that the interest rate can increase after the initial five-year period.

Chapter 8

Fixed Mortgages

There are three basic choices you will have when mortgaging your property—fixed, adjustable, or hybrid mortgages. There are variations of each. This chapter discusses the fixed mortgage, Chapter 9 discusses the adjustable mortgage, and Chapter 10 discusses hybrid mortgages.

The fixed interest rate mortgage (FIRM) is the traditional way to finance a home. At one time, it was the only mortgage offered by most lenders. It is also the easiest to understand because there are no changes over the life of the loan. A FIRM has a set rate of interest requiring an equal payment for a specific number of years. Future fluctuation of interest rates has no bearing on the loan.

Example: If you have a 30-year loan at 7% interest with a $1000 per month payment, that is it. You will pay $1000 per month every month for thirty years. Your interest rate will always be 7%. Even if you may make additional payments to reduce what you owe in order to pay the loan off sooner, your interest rate and payment amount will remain the same.

When interest rates are low and you expect to keep your property for many years, it is the best loan you can get.

Why is the Interest Rate Always a Little Higher?

The problem with fixed-rate loans is the lender's problem. Interest rates may increase over the years, but not for your loan. Because of this, lenders will structure your loan to protect themselves.

They will charge a higher rate of interest, and in many instances, higher fees than if you got a loan with an interest rate that would change (adjust) as market rates changed.

A way of reducing the higher rate is by using a *buydown*. By paying more discount points, you can get a lower interest rate.

> **Example:** You have just sold your home and have $70,000 cash. The new home that you are going to buy only requires a $50,000 down payment. You do not trust yourself not to spend the other $20,000. You now have a choice. You can pay a larger down payment and reduce the amount that you borrow, reducing your monthly payment, or you could choose to buy down the interest rate to reduce your monthly payment.

Your decision will be based on how long you intend to pay on the loan. There are too many different possibilities to cover here. Ask your real estate agent or financial advisor to figure out which is best depending on your specific situation. As discussed, the most important factor is to be realistic as to how long you will keep the property.

There are other considerations besides the interest rate. The cost of the loan (points and fees) will also figure into the mathematical equation as to how many years it will take to make up the additional costs of the fixed-rate loan.

The final consideration is the market. Looking at the market conditions for the latter part of 2004, you would have the following factors to consider.

- Interest rates are at historic lows.
- The country is out of recession and there is job growth.
- The price of oil is high and this creates higher prices for goods and services.

• The Federal Reserve Board, fearing inflation, has raised rates several times in recent months, which has not yet substantially affected rates for new mortgages.

These signs seem to point to higher future interest rates. How much higher and how fast the rates will rise is not known. Lenders also see these signs and price the difference between fixed rates and adjustable rates accordingly. If you are pessimistic and believe rates will raise quickly, you want the fixed-rate loan. If you think the high oil prices will cause another recession and the rates will remain stable or even go down, maybe the adjustable is right for you. With its lower initial rate and the length of time it may take to adjust to a level higher than the fixed mortgage (plus taking into consideration your savings over the time period when the adjustable rate was lower than the fixed rate), this can offer significant savings in the short run.

There is an advantage to a fixed-rate loan that does not show by just comparing numbers. A fixed-rate loan gives you peace of mind. If rates go up, you are safe. If rates go down, you refinance. Unless you are fairly sure that you will not be in your home five years from now, you are usually better off to get the fixed-rate loan. Here is the problem: you plan to move in five years, so you get an adjustable rate loan. However, rates increase substantially. You now are ready to move up to your next home, which is bigger and more expensive. With the higher prevailing rates, you may no longer qualify or it may be just a bad time to get a new loan.

The decision as to whether to get a fixed or adjustable loan gets harder. There are not just adjustable loans, but combination or hybrid loans that are fixed for a period of years and then adjust. There are also adjustable loans that will rise or fall quickly and ones that will react much slower to rate changes. As these loans are discussed later, you will see that there are many factors to take into consideration when deciding between the different loan options.

Things to Know

Most fixed-rate loans are not assumable. They will contain a *due on sale* clause. This clause will say that if you sell your property, you must pay off your loan. They may also contain a prepayment penalty. This protects the lender against falling interest rates, since you are most likely to pay off the loan by refinancing if rates drop dramatically.

An important question to ask about any loan concerns making additional principal payments. An additional principal payment means that you pay more than the required amount of your monthly payment. This extra money reduces what you owe. It does not go to lessen next month's payment. Since your interest amount is based on what you owe (your declining balance), you will pay less interest on future payments.

> ### From the Expert
> Be sure you know how much you can prepay without penalty, as well as the penalty for a complete payoff.

Prepayment penalties can cover additional payments as well as paying off the loan in full. For example, this prevents you from quickly paying down your $200,000 loan to $50,000 and then making only required payments.

Another question you should ask is how much extra you can pay each month. Before the computer, lenders required that you pay additional principal payments in specified increments, such as a double payment or $100 increments. Since the computer can figure out whether you paid $100 extra or $3.57 extra without difficulty, there is no longer a reason for increments. If your lender requires specific increments, it will make additional payments more difficult for you.

Additional principal payments are especially important when rates are high. For example, on a $100,000, 30-year loan, with a rate of 8.5%, an additional principal payment of $25 per month would reduce the term from thirty years to twenty-six years, three months. An additional monthly payment of $75 would reduce it to just over twenty-one years, six months.

Even when rates are low, it helps. A $25 additional payment on a 5.5%, $100,000 loan would reduce the term to twenty-seven years. Additional principal payments are examined more closely in Chapter 12.

Chapter 9

Adjustable Rate Mortgages

The *adjustable rate mortgage* (ARM) is the favorite of most lenders. From the lender's point of view, it is the mortgage that is fair to all parties — it changes to reflect current market conditions. As interest rates rise and fall, the interest rate of your mortgage follows suit.

To understand ARMs, you must understand the language used with them. The interest rate of the loan is tied to an index. An *index* is an interest rate that is publicly published, such as the interest paid on a government bill or note, the cost of funds for a Federal Reserve Bank district, the prime rate, and so on.

The interest rate on your loan may be higher than the index rate. For example, it could be 2% over the rate of the index used. You may have heard phrases such as *2% over prime,* which means the lender is using the prime rate index and charging 2% over it for the loan. The amount over the index rate is called the *margin.*

Your protection against skyrocketing interest rates is called a *ceiling,* or more commonly, a *cap.* For example, if your original interest rate is 5% and your cap is 5%, your rate can never go higher than 10%. You should also have a cap on an adjustment. This means that your rate cannot be raised by, for example, more than 1% per year (or whatever period is used for adjustments).

Indexes

One of the most important features of an adjustable rate mortgage is the *index* to which it is tied. If you plan to keep your loan for more than five years, it may be the most important feature, as all indexes do not react equally to rate changes.

There are two basic types of indexes. They are classified as *leading* and *lagging*. As the names imply, leading indexes react quickly to economic changes and are highly volatile. Lagging indexes adjust more slowly and do not reach the highs and lows of the leading indexes. Some of the indexes used to determine adjustable mortgage rates include the following.

- Constant Maturity Treasury (CMT)
- Treasury Bill (T-Bill)
- 12-month Treasury Average (MTA)
- Cost of Deposit Index (CODI)
- 11th District Cost of Funds Index (COFI)
- Cost of Savings Index (COSI)
- London Inter Bank Offering Rate (LIBOR)
- Certificates of Deposit (CD) Indexes
- Prime Rate

To use an extreme historical example, in May 1981, the prime rate soared to 20.50%. The cost of funds index had also risen, but only to 11.43%. By May 1986, the prime rate had fallen to 8.25%, a 12.25% drop. The Cost of Funds index had also fallen, but only to 8.44%, a 2.99% drop. A mortgage lender's success is largely dependent on interest rate trends, especially if making portfolio loans. A lender selling loans to secondary lenders will not worry about rate changes five years from now. The lender making a portfolio loan will usually want to use a leading index. If rates rise, the increase is reflected quickly in the loan rate. If rates fall, it is less likely that the borrower will refinance and the lender will lose the loan entirely.

> ### From the Expert
> When interest rates are at historic highs, a leading index may be to the borrower's advantage. When rates are low, the lagging index is preferred.

Your decision depends primarily on the length of time that you intend to keep the loan. If you are planning to keep the loan for five years or less, you are probably better off to get the lowest interest rate available, even if it is tied to a leading index. Your protection is the cap on adjustments. The risk of the loan adjusting dramatically and unexpectedly in a five-year period is usually outweighed by the lower interest rate being offered. The longer you keep the loan, the greater the risk. This is especially true if the trend appears to be toward higher rates.

The advice is simple. If you plan to keep your loan for an indefinite period over five years and you believe interest rates will rise, get a fixed interest rate loan. If you only qualify for an adjustable rate loan, get one that uses a lagging index. The lagging index is most often the best for the borrower under any interest rate trend. If rates rise, they rise more slowly. If rates fall, you can refinance.

Something to remember when trying to estimate how long you will keep your mortgage: If your plan is to sell your property in a few years and buy a more expensive home, rising rates may prevent this by making the payments on the more expensive home beyond your reach. Also, refinancing may not be an option if rates rise, since you will have to pay the prevailing higher rate at the time you try to refinance. Planning to keep your mortgage only a few years because that is how long you usually stay in one place before your job requires you to move is a much better reason.

The following is a list of the most often used indexes and a short explanation of each. When you are offered an adjustable rate mortgage, ask your lender which index is being used and how it has reacted to economic changes over the last few years compared to other indexes. You can also do your own research by typing "mortgage indexes" into a search engine. There are several good websites that will list current index rates, as well as supply historical data.

- *Constant Maturity Treasury* (CMT) *indexes.* These indexes are the weekly or monthly average yields on U.S. Treasury securities, and are based on closing market bids for actively traded Treasury securities. It is a quick reacting leading index. As of December 2004, the rate ranged from 2.67% on the 1-year security to 3.60% on the 5-year

security. Checking the current rate may give you an indication of the direction in which rates are moving.

- *London Inter Bank Offering Rate* (LIBOR). The average interest rate of deposits of Euros traded among banks in London. The LIBOR is also considered a leading index, adjusting quickly to world economic changes. As of December 2004, the LIBOR Index ranged from 2.41% for the 1-month rate to 3.10% for the 1-year rate.
- *11th District Cost of Funds Index* (COFI). This index is based more on interest paid on savings and checking accounts. As you know, the interest paid by savings institutions on these accounts rises at a slower rate than loan rates. The 11th District encompasses the savings institutions (savings and loan associations and savings banks) head-quartered in Arizona, California, and Nevada. The rate is more commonly used in the Western states, but is not confined to use there. It is a lagging index that moves at a much slower rate than either the CMT or LIBOR, and rarely reaches their extremes.
- *Prime Rate*. The prime rate has historically been the rate banks charge their best customers for short-term loans. It is now also being used as a common index for equity lines of credit. Some lenders are offering rates below prime for equity lines with low loan-to-value ratios for customers with high credit scores. The prime rate will move on Federal Reserve Board interest rate hikes, and generally reflects the Fed's view of the strength of the economy and the threat of inflation. In times of high inflation, the prime rate can rise quickly, since the Federal Reserve Board members seem to consider inflation the greatest threat to our country's economic health.

There are several other indexes that are not as commonly used. If you are getting an adjustable rate mortgage loan, be sure to question the lender about the index being used and its volatility.

Margins

The *margin* is the difference between the index interest rate and the rate charged the borrower. The lender has no control over the index rate, but complete control of the margin. One lender could set the interest rate at

2% over COFI, while another could charge 4% over COFI. Shopping for a lender that uses the index most suitable to your situation *and* the lowest margin is crucial to getting the best adjustable loan.

Start Rate

Many adjustable rate loans offer a *start rate*. This is a very low rate that lasts for only a short time (usually three to six months) before your actual interest rate begins.

Start rates are not only confusing and misleading—they are, in many instances, a scam. A lender offering a start rate as low as 2% cannot get the money to lend to you at that rate. This means that the lender is taking a loss for the first few months of your loan. Lenders are not in business to lose money.

A start rate is similar to a retail store offering a specific item at a cost so low that they lose money selling it. This is called a *loss leader*. The idea is that when you come to the store to buy the item, you will buy other items that are profitable. The difference between the loss

> **From the Expert**
>
> While the start rate may seem to be for your benefit, lenders use it to their advantage.

leader and the start rate is that you can buy only the loss leader item and leave the store. You cannot get the start rate only. You have to take the profitable part of the loan as well.

There are several advantages of a low start rate to the lender, especially the less-than-honest lender. First, it is a wonderful advertising gimmick. The naïve borrower hears only the words 2% *mortgage loan*. This is exactly the type of borrower that this lender wants—someone who can be sold a very profitable loan.

Another advantage is that the lender can qualify the borrower at the start rate. This is good for getting the loan, but puts many borrowers in over their heads when the true payments have to be made. To prevent this, lenders often connect the payment increase to the start-rate payment. When the interest rate jumps to the real rate, the payment does not increase to cover it, also putting the borrower in a poorer financial position.

Example: Your start rate is 2%, requiring a payment of $2000 per month. After a few months, the rate becomes 2% over the one year Treasury Bill index, for a total interest rate of 6%. The adjustment on the payment is a maximum of 7.5%.

On a $300,000 loan, an interest rate increase of 4% is $12,000 per year, or $1000 per month. The payment increases by 7.5% to $1300 per month, a shortfall of $700 per month.

Since the borrower is not paying enough interest to reduce the principal balance, the interest owed but not paid is added to the principal. This creates negative amortization. Now the borrower is no longer reducing the term of the loan. Since the principal balance is increasing, the borrower is now paying compound interest.

At some point in time, the loan must be repaid. This can be done by an increase in the monthly payments necessary to amortize the loan, creating an extreme burden on the borrower, or by a balloon payment that would necessitate refinancing. This may not be possible, since much more money is owed than was originally borrowed. Even if it all works out because the borrower is becoming financially stronger and home prices are increasing, there was a major risk and major expense over a more sensible loan.

There can be a good use of a start rate to qualify a buyer if the start rate is closer to the real rate and the payment adjustment enables the borrower to at least pay the interest once the loan adjusts to the permanent rate formula. Then the payment can gradually adjust to an amount that pays on the principal.

Understanding ARMs

The best way to understand an adjustable rate loan is to look at a specific example, and then, using made-up numbers, examine some variations.

Example: The terms of the loan are as follows. It has a start rate of 2% interest. After six months, the rate changes to 5%. The 5% rate is the rate of the Federal Reserve 11th District Cost of Funds (the index

for this example) of 3% plus a 2% margin. The cap is 5%, so you can never pay more than 10% interest. Some lenders will say that the cap is 10% when explaining this loan. Always ask if they define the cap as the total interest that can be required or the amount of the increase. The adjustment period is six months. The adjustment cap is 1%.

Every six months, you must look at the current rate of the index. The interest rate rises or falls by the same amount as the rise or fall of the index rate, up to the cap of 1% per six-month period.

This is where the first problem arises. If the interest rate goes up, does your monthly payment also go up? The answer is a definite maybe. Depending on the terms of your specific loan, you may have an increase in your monthly payment that fully reflects the increased interest, partially reflects the increased interest, or does not change at all.

If you owe $300,000, a 1% rise in interest is $3000 per year. That is $250 per month. This may strain your budget. If your payment increases by less than $250, you are not paying down your loan as quickly as you anticipated. If your payment does not increase at all, you could quickly be paying interest only or less (negative amortization). You can voluntarily increase your monthly payments to avoid this, but can you afford it?

You can easily see that timing is critical for an adjustable loan. If interest rates are at historic highs when you get your loan, your rate will probably adjust downward. An added bonus is that falling interest rates usually cause an increase in property values.

If you use an adjustable loan when rates are at historic lows, you will probably see your rate go up. One problem is that rising interest rates usually cause property values to stabilize or fall. In an extreme case, you can no longer afford to make your increased monthly payment, and falling property prices make you unable to sell.

The logical question is, "Why would anyone want an adjustable loan when interest rates are low?" The major reason is that it is the only way

to qualify. The formula used to qualify a buyer for a loan considers the beginning monthly payment, not the possible future monthly payments. It is similar to the interest-only loan situation with the balloon payment. If it is the only way to home ownership, you take the risk.

A more sound reason would be that your job requires you to move every few years. You will pay lower interest and fees for the adjustable loan and you will probably sell before the rates change too much.

Flexible Payment Adjustable Rate Mortgage

A lender may suggest a *flexible payment adjustable rate mortgage*, which limits the payment increase in order to ease the borrower's fears. The flexible payment aspect of the loan looks like a solution to the problem. The typical loan of this type will call for a payment adjustment of no more than 7.5% per year, based on the start rate payment. However, there are two problems with this loan for the borrower.

First, the increased payment will usually not be enough to cover interest only (negative amortization). This is especially true in a market in which the index rate is rising. Remember, the margin is part of the interest rate. A high margin will cause negative amortization even if the index rate is stable or falls slightly.

In flexible payment adjustable rate mortgages, there is a clause that if the negative amortization reaches a certain level — usually no more than 125% of the original loan amount — the payment will be adjusted to amortize the loan, superceding the payment cap. Since you owe more than you originally borrowed and have less time to pay it off, the payment will be even higher than if you originally agreed to fully amortize the loan over the original loan term.

The second problem is that the loan will be *recast* periodically, commonly every five years. Recasting means that the payment is adjusted to fully amortize the loan in the remaining time of the term. This recasting clause also supercedes the yearly payment cap and adjusts the payment to whatever is necessary to pay off the loan in the remaining term.

What is the answer? It is the same old story of common sense. If the start rate and initial monthly payment are far below prevailing rates and

the payment amount necessary to amortize the loan amount in the agreed upon term, be careful. You know how much you are borrowing. You know the real interest rate that you will have to pay (the index plus the margin). You know how many years you have to pay it off (the term).

From the Expert
It is not difficult to avoid payment shock. Some simple figuring on your own will tell you what to expect. As a result, you will be less likely to get caught in the trap of deciding if this type of loan is good for you.

What does common sense tell you? The less you pay in the early years of the loan, the more you will have to pay later. It also tells you that the smaller the payment, the less will go to principal. This means that you will pay much more interest than the price of the early smaller payments.

Studies done on these loans show increases in the monthly payment well over 100%, even if the index rises only slightly. The higher the margin and the lower the start rate, the greater the payment increase. It has been suggested that lenders be required to raise the start rate based on their margins. A lender with a 4% margin would be required to have a higher start rate compared to a lender with a 2% margin. This would narrow the gap between the initial required payment and the adjusted payment if maximum negative amortization occurs, or when the loan is recast. However, there is currently no law or regulation requiring lenders to do this.

Again, the time element is very important. If your income does not allow for a standard payment, interest rates are high and are expected to fall, housing prices are on the rise, and you plan to sell the home within five years, this may be a great loan. Unfortunately, most of these *ifs* are unpredictable.

The smarter way is to work out a somewhat pessimistic scenario of the possibilities. If you believe you can survive the worst case and the only loan that will allow you to buy the house is one with a low start rate and high margin, you at least are making an informed decision.

Chapter 10

Hybrid Mortgages

Hybrid loans fall between a fixed-rate and adjustable-rate loan. Lenders realized that there was a market for borrowers who wanted the lower cost of an adjustable loan, but were afraid of a possible interest rate increase within a short time. The lenders also realized that some interest rate adjustment was better than none at all.

The hybrid mortgage loan begins with a fixed rate for a set time. The most common fixed periods are three, five, seven, and ten years. At the end of the fixed term, the loan adjusts to the agreed-upon index rate plus the margin. Further adjustment is most commonly yearly, although the adjustment period may be every three, or even every five, years.

The loans are categorized by their overall term, then fixed term, then adjustment period. A 30-year loan with a 3-year fixed term and a 1-year adjustment period would be expressed as a 30/3/1 loan. A 15-year loan with a 5-year fixed term and an adjustment period every 3 years would be expressed as a 15/5/3 loan.

At the end of the fixed interest period, the loan is recalculated to reflect the new interest rate. If you borrowed $100,000 on a 30/3/1 loan, for example, the loan would be recalculated at the end of three years. Your payment would be based on the new interest rate (index rate plus margin), term remaining (twenty-seven years), and the principal balance ($100,000, less the amount of principal paid during the first three years). Each succeeding year would have an interest rate adjustment based on a change in the index rate, with a resulting payment adjustment.

There are some advantages to the hybrid mortgage loan.

- The fixed interest rate period is at a lower rate than a fixed-rate loan for the entire term. If you expect to sell your home during the fixed-rate period, it equates to getting a fixed-rate loan at a lower rate.
- The risk of a higher rate is postponed for three to ten years rather than three months to one year with a standard adjustable rate mortgage. This gives you time to increase your income or savings should the new rate require a substantially higher payment.
- Many hybrid loans are assumable, which may be an advantage if you sell the property.

However, there also are some disadvantages to the hybrid mortgage loan.

- The initial interest rate on a hybrid loan is higher than on an adjustable rate loan.
- The new rate at the end of the fixed-rate period may cause a significant increase in the monthly payment.
- Once the interest rate begins to adjust, it could be more costly that a fixed-rate loan would have been.

As with most mortgage loans, there are several factors to consider.

- *Interest rate.* Is the lower rate for the hybrid enough to make it worthwhile compared to a fixed-rate loan? If you plan to stay in the home for the foreseeable future, you may want to compare the hybrid to a shorter term fixed-rate loan that has a lower interest rate.
- *Loan costs.* A lower interest rate does little good if you are being charged points and other fees that eat up the savings. Comparing several lenders' programs will help you determine the standard costs.
- *Index.* As you know from Chapter 9, there are leading and lagging indexes. If you are concerned about rate increases, find a lender using a lagging index, such as COFI.
- *Margin.* The lender's profit will be the fixed part of your interest rate once the loan adjusts. Margins can range from .5% to 4% or higher.

Get several quotes from lenders. There may be substantial differences in margin amounts, which can also be negotiated.

- *Prepayment penalty.* If you plan to pay off the loan before adjustment begins, a prepayment penalty may eliminate any savings from a lower interest rate.
- *Caps.* There are three caps to protect you from fast rising interest rates.

> **From the Expert**
>
> If you feel that you are being overcharged, do not hesitate to tell your lender or mortgage broker that you believe you should get a better margin rate. Ask for an explanation as to why the rate is so high.

First is the *lifetime cap*. A 5% loan with a 5% lifetime cap means that you will never pay more than 10% interest. Second is the *interest rate adjustment cap*. How much can the rate adjust during any one adjustment period? This is extremely important. It is your security that you can count on a maximum that the rate can adjust and plan for this increase in a rising interest rate market. The third cap is the *payment cap*. Will any interest rate adjustment be fully reflected in your monthly payment? If the answer is yes, you should figure out what your monthly payment will be if the interest rate adjusts to the highest rate allowed. If the answer is no, will you be able to extend the term of your loan or will you have a balloon payment?

Finally, you must look at the worst possible adjustment. For example, your fixed rate is 5% for three years. There is a 5% cap. The worst that could happen is that three years from now, your interest rate will be 10%. If you owe $240,000 when the loan becomes adjustable, that is a $12,000 per year increase in interest. Will your payment increase by $1000 per month?

Refinancing will not be a good option, since prevailing rates for a new loan will be in the same 10% range. Since fast rising interest rates usually drive down property values, you may not be able to get out from under by selling.

Of course, you can *what if* yourself out of buying a home. If the only way you can qualify for any home is through a hybrid, the gamble is probably worth it. If the hybrid is the only way to buy your *dream* home, maybe you should look again at the lower-priced *adequate* home that you could keep if the worst happens to interest rates.

You can plan to minimize a larger increase in interest rates, but the problem is it requires discipline that most people do not have. If you can take the amount of money you save every month with your lower interest hybrid loan and put it into some sort of interest-bearing account, you can create a cushion for yourself for when the loan switches from fixed to adjustable.

> **Example:** By getting the hybrid at a lower interest rate, you save $100 per month over a fixed-rate mortgage. Your loan will begin to adjust after five years. Each month, you put this $100 savings into an interest-bearing account. At the end of five years, you will have $6000, plus the amount of interest you have accumulated. This can be used to pay the monthly increase in your payment or give you some time during which to find a buyer if you cannot afford the higher payment.

The higher your loan, the greater the savings. On a $200,000 loan, a 1% difference in interest would save you $2000 per year. You would have $10,000 at the end of five years, plus the interest you made on the savings. It may put a strain on your budget, but might also avoid disaster if the worst happens. Of course, if interest rates do not increase, having an extra $10,000 in the bank cannot hurt.

Chapter 11

Jumbo Loans

As the name implies, a *jumbo* loan is a loan for a large amount of money. A loan is a jumbo if it exceeds the maximum amount of Fannie Mae and Freddie Mac programs. Because exceeding the loan amount allowed by Fannie Mae and Freddie Mac guidelines means that the loan does not *conform* to the guidelines, the jumbo is also called a *nonconforming loan*.

There is no one standard amount that defines a loan as jumbo, since Fannie Mae and Freddie Mac change their maximums yearly based on changes of real estate prices. As of January 2005, the highest allowable amount for a single family property mortgage loan in the continental United States was $359,650. Anything above that amount was considered jumbo. This amount will change as real estate prices rise or fall.

Loan programs for jumbo mortgage loans are as varied as smaller loans. There are fixed-rate, adjustable, and hybrid jumbos. The loan-to-value can be anywhere up to 100%. The term is also the same as smaller mortgage loans, the most common being fifteen and thirty years. A jumbo loan can be used to purchase or refinance a primary residence, vacation home, or investment property.

The strength of the borrower will determine the interest rate, just as with smaller loans. For equally qualified

> **From the Expert**
>
> Although there is no real distinction, some lenders are classifying loans over $650,000 as *super jumbo loans* and offering special programs for these higher amount loans.

borrowers, the jumbo will have a higher rate—usually between .125% and .75%—than a conforming loan, depending on down payment and the lender's profit requirements.

Although the exact number varies with the lender, some lenders are using the terms *good credit* and *excellent credit* in their underwriting for jumbo loans. Excellent credit may get the borrower a lower interest rate or require less documentation than good credit. Generally, good credit would range from a FICO score of 650 to 700, and excellent credit would be above 700.

If you are thinking of buying a home that will require a jumbo mortgage, you are faced with the same challenges that you would face for a smaller loan. Research to find the right lender offering the right program for you must be done for any mortgage loan.

A good website to use for additional information is that of Countrywide Financial at **www.countrywide.com**. This site gives lots of information on different types of loans without requiring you to give them any information.

Avoiding the Jumbo Loan

A big disadvantage to the jumbo loan is that even a slightly higher interest rate over a conforming loan is magnified because of the large amount being borrowed. There is a way around this if you need a loan slightly higher than the maximum conforming limits. Many lenders now offer a conforming loan for the maximum allowed and a second mortgage loan for the balance needed. Since you are saving interest on the higher amount first mortgage, you can afford to pay a higher rate on the second and still come out ahead.

> **Example:** Since conforming loan maximums change with the real estate market and region, suppose $250,000 is the conforming loan limit. You need to borrow $260,000. Instead of paying the higher interest of a jumbo loan, you get a second loan for $10,000. Since the higher interest of the jumbo would be paid on $260,000, the savings are considerable. You could pay over 15% interest on the second

(you should not have to) and still come out ahead, using a difference between the rates of a jumbo and conforming loan of only .25%, with interest on the conforming loan at 7%.

Chapter 12

Prepayment

This book has touched on prepayment with plans such as biweekly payments, but the subject is important enough to deserve its own chapter. Prepayment of your mortgage loan has two purposes. One is to shorten the term. The other is to pay less interest.

The way prepayment was traditionally made was by paying the exact amount of principal on your next payment along with your current payment. If you had 300 payments left on your loan, your current payment would bring you down to 299. If you paid payment 300 plus the principal reduction amount on payment 299 at the same time, you would now have 298 payments remaining.

This was an easy way to figure out how much to pay and how many months you would have to pay to pay off the loan. The greatest advantage in prepaying was during the early years of your loan. This was when the amount going to principal was lowest and the interest amount was highest. If your payment was $1000 per month early in your loan, perhaps only $100 was going to principal and $900 to interest on your current payment. Your next payment might have $110 going to principal. By prepaying the $110, you saved $890 in interest.

Late in your loan the opposite would be true. $900 would go to principal and $100 to interest. You would have to make a very large additional principal payment to save a small amount of interest. It simply was not a good option.

Changes that Affect Prepayments Today

There are two major changes that affect prepayment today. The first is the computer. The reason you were required to pay the exact amount of principal as a prepayment was that someone had to figure it out. Unless you used this easy method, it was very time-consuming for the lender to redo your whole amortization schedule. The computer refigures the schedule in seconds, making the amount of the prepayment immaterial.

The second change makes prepayment even more important for some loans. In the *old days* you had to put 20% of the loan amount as a down payment and there was no PMI. Today, loans greater than 80% loan-to-value are common and PMI is required. Prepaying a loan down to 80% not only saves interest, but allows you to stop paying PMI.

If you are paying PMI and have some money available at the end of the month, making additional principal payments is an excellent investment. Unfortunately, most borrowers who do not have 20% to put down do not have extra money with which to make prepayments in the early years of the loan. However, there are other, more sophisticated, methods to eliminating PMI.

> **Example 1:** You originally got a 90% loan and you have paid it down to 85%. Your income has increased, so you now have a few hundred dollars that you could put into prepayments. Your home has probably also increased in value. You should be able to get an equity line of credit at a lower rate than your current mortgage rate. You could use the line of credit to pay your loan down to 80% and eliminate the PMI. Then you would use the extra money you have to make payments on the line of credit loan.

> **Example 2:** You have purchased a home for $200,000 and put 10% down. Your monthly payment on your $180,000, 30-year loan at 6% interest is $1,079.19 (rounded to $1,080). You have paid down your loan to $170,000 by making required payments, but still need to reduce it by another $10,000 to eliminate the PMI.

If you were to get an equity line of credit for $10,000 and use the money to pay down your first mortgage, you could eliminate the PMI and save the interest that you would have paid to reduce the loan by making required monthly payments. By making the required payments you would reduce your loan balance to $160,000 in 39 months and pay over $32,000 in interest for that period. In addition, you would pay a PMI premium of approximately $75 per month, or $2925, for a total cost to you of approximately $35,000.

A reasonable interest rate for an equity line of credit would be less than the interest on your first mortgage loan. If we use a rate of 5% on a 5-year loan, your monthly payment would be $188.71 ($189). Since you eliminated the $75 per month PMI, your out-of-pocket payment would be $114 per month. If you made only the required monthly payment, your total cost would be $11,340. The total interest paid would be $1,340.

You can see the obvious advantages, but there are also risks. First, by getting an additional loan, you are taking on an additional required payment. If you have future financial difficulties, this could become a burden. Second, the equity line of credit may only be available with an adjustable rate. This could raise your payment amount if rates increase and lessen the advantage. Both risks seem manageable and well worth taking to realize the savings.

The last consideration for our example is what else you could do with the $114 per month. There is no safe investment in today's market that equals a rate of return even close to prepaying your mortgage loan, especially if you eliminate the PMI payment.

Another possibility is to borrow against your 401(k). This is usually not a good idea for several reasons.

- You are borrowing from yourself. The money you borrow will not be earning retirement income for you. Since many plans have employer contributions, this could be a significant loss.

- If you leave your job, you may have to pay back the loan in full. This could cause you to stay with your current employer and pass up a better opportunity.
- Under current law, you will have five years to pay back the loan. If you fail to do so, you will incur a penalty of 10% of the amount owed, plus you will have to pay income tax on that amount.

Chapter 13

Government Loans

There are two types of government mortgage loans that must be addressed—FHA loans and VA loans. Farm loans are not discussed, as they are specialized, and if you are looking to finance the purchase of a farm, you should seek advice from your local bank.

The government mortgage loans are not really loans from the government. Instead, a government agency *insures* or *guarantees* a loan made by a private lender. These are loans insured by the Federal Housing Administration (FHA) or guaranteed by the Department of Veterans Affairs (VA).

The purpose of these governmental programs is to facilitate home ownership for those moderate or low income families who do not have the ability—usually the down payment—to qualify for a conventional loan. The insurance or guarantee takes away the lenders' risk of loss, allowing them to make loans with as little as 3% down for FHA insured loans and zero down for VA guaranteed loans.

FHA Insured Mortgage Loans

The Federal Housing Administration (FHA) does not make loans, but insures the lender against loss that may occur if the property is foreclosed upon and the sale does not cover the amount owed. FHA insures lenders against loss from making loans that have a higher risk of default than the lender would accept without the insurance. For purposes of simplicity

and because of its common terminology, these FHA insured loans are referred to as FHA loans.

The FHA Advantage

The major advantage to the borrower has changed in recent years. At one time, the low down payment was the major advantage. Today, many lenders offer conventional mortgage loans of up to a 100% loan-to-value ratio.

The difference is in qualifying. FHA standards for approving a borrower for loans requiring little or no down payment are more liberal than those of conventional lenders. FHA will accept credit problems that most conventional lenders will not, such as a recent bankruptcy. A borrower who has been discharged from Chapter 7 bankruptcy (debts are eliminated) for two years is eligible for an FHA loan. A Chapter 13 bankruptcy (bankrupt person agrees to pay debts on a revised schedule) requires a discharge only one year old.

> **From the Expert**
>
> Since the purpose of FHA loans is to allow more people to buy homes, it makes sense that the standards for qualifying borrowers are low.

When qualifying a borrower's income, FHA allows co-borrowers who do not occupy the property to have their income count in the qualification process. FHA also allows gifts for closing costs that conventional lenders would not.

Disadvantages

There are three major disadvantages to FHA loans.

First, there is a mortgage limit that excludes many homes. The lending limit is set by area, with higher limits in states with higher home costs. The nationwide average as of January 2005 was about $160,000. The limit for California, a state where homes generally cost more, was about $310,000 in the highest priced counties. The median price of a California home at this time, however, was well over $350,000. You can see the problem.

You must remember that the purpose of these loans is to allow low-income borrowers a chance at home ownership. Low-income borrowers buy the least expensive homes. They may cost less because of size, location, need for repair, or a combination of these factors.

The second disadvantage is that selling a home to a buyer using an FHA-insured loan may cost the seller more money than if the buyer used conventional financing. The seller may be asked to pay points, which is allowed under FHA rules. This does not happen with conventional financing. This was a more serious problem when the buyer was allowed by law to pay only one point. The FHA buyer may now pay the points. The time involved is longer to close than conventional loans. Even with automated underwriting and more authority given to lenders to qualify borrowers, it still could take forty-five days to process an FHA loan. Sellers will accept a buyer who will finance conventionally over an FHA buyer.

The third disadvantage to FHA loans is the mortgage insurance premium (MIP). This is the FHA equivalent of the conventional loan's PMI (private mortgage insurance). The cost for MIP is higher than PMI.

> **From the Expert**
>
> The MIP makes the recently introduced 100% loans (discussed later) cost less, even though the interest rate may be higher.

FHA insured loans work best for low-priced homes when the buyer cannot get conventional financing. When there are many buyers and few homes for sale (a *seller's market*), fewer homes are sold FHA. When there are few buyers and many homes for sale (a *buyer's market*), more FHA financing is used.

The advice is simple. If you can qualify for a conventional loan at a standard rate, you are better off than getting an FHA loan. If you must pay a substandard (higher) interest rate, higher points, and so on because of credit or income problems, FHA may be your answer to home ownership.

FHA Programs

There are four major FHA programs of which you should be aware.

1. *203 (b).* This is the original program, which has been used since the depression of the 1930s. It is aimed at borrowers who would not qualify for conventional financing because of credit, income, or cash requirements. The borrower must intend to use the home as his or her primary residence. It requires a 3% down payment and allows closing costs and mortgage insurance to be financed. It covers one to four family homes.

2. *203 (k).* This program is for rehabilitation of property. The main goal is to revitalize neighborhoods that have properties in need of rehabilitation. It is very broad, covering property that has one to four family units, condominiums, and even property that is partly commercial. It even covers complete demolition and rebuilding, as well as moving a building onto the land after demolition. (There are requirements for keeping the original foundation.) The difference from conventional financing is that one loan can cover the purchase and rehabilitation, based on the estimated value of the property after the work is completed. As with all FHA loans, qualifying is easier than for a conventional loan.

3. *234 (c).* The purpose of the program is to help tenants buy units when their apartments are converted to condominiums. It can also be used by developers to convert apartments to condominiums. Qualification similar to 203 (b) is required.

4. *251.* This is the FHA adjustable rate mortgage program. It can be used in conjunction with the three programs described above. The index used is the *Constant Maturity Treasury* (CMT). The adjustment is yearly with a 1% cap, and the lifetime cap is 5%.

There are several other programs that are highly specific and should be looked into if you qualify. Programs like the 184 program covering Indian tribal lands require special procedures from both the tribe and the Bureau of Indian Affairs. Details can be obtained from:

Office of Loan Guarantee
National Office of Native American Programs
1999 Broadway
Suite 3390
Denver, CO 80202
303-675-1600
800-561-5913

Other programs of interest, such as the *Officer Next Door* (OND) and *Teacher Next Door* (TND) programs, are especially designed to provide home ownership for those having a specific occupation. These are coordinated with local governments or nonprofit corporations. They allow a police officer or teacher to buy a HUD-owned property at up to a 50% discount. The programs also provide second mortgages to cover down payments and closing costs. If the borrower lives in the property for three years, the loans do not have to be repaid. For additional information, contact:

U.S. Department of HUD
c/o Morris-Griffin/First Madison Services, Inc.
4111 South Darlington
Suite 300
Tulsa, Oklahoma 74135
800-967-3050

NOTE: *You can also type a category such as "teacher's mortgages" or "mortgages for police" into a search engine. The special loans and grants will be described on websites you may find. Read the information carefully. Some of the websites are just lenders who want to make ordinary loans and want to make you believe that they are offering you something special.*

Visit HUD's website at **www.hud.gov** for all program details and lending limits for your area. You can also get a list of HUD-approved brokers (those who list HUD owned properties that are for sale) and HUD-approved

lenders for FHA insured loans. There is also a list of HUD-approved counselors to consult if you have an FHA loan and face foreclosure.

VA Loans

The VA loan program began after World War II to help veterans buy homes. The FHA *insures* a lender against loss, while the VA *guarantees* a lender against loss. The difference between insurance and guarantee does not affect the borrower. These are differences in the procedure that a lender must follow to be reimbursed for a loss. (The following is the procedural difference as explained by HUD.)

- *VA – When a delinquency is reported to VA, and no realistic alternative to foreclosure is developed by the loan holder or through VA's supplemental servicing of the loan, VA determines, through an economic analysis, whether VA will (a) authorize the holder to convey the property, securing the VA Loan to the Secretary of Veterans Affairs following termination or (b) pay the loan guaranty amount to the holder. The decision as to disposition of properties securing defaulted VA Loans is made on a case-by-case basis, using the procedures set forth in 38 U.S.C. Section 3732(c), as amended.*
- *FHA – Upon default, the lender – depending upon the circumstances – may (a) assign the mortgage to FHA, (b) acquire (through foreclosure or deed in lieu of foreclosure) and convey title to FHA, or (c) work with the borrower to sell the property before the foreclosure sale. The lender will receive insurance benefits equal to the unpaid principal balance of the loan, plus approved expenses.*

The original program had two main goals. First was to make it easy for veterans to buy a home by not requiring a down payment. Second was to protect veterans from overpayment. In order to accomplish this, the rules were that the buyer could pay no more than the appraised value of the property. The appraisal, called a *certificate of reasonable value* (CRV) was done by a VA approved appraiser. There was also a maximum interest rate that could

be charged, as well as a restriction on points. Today, the no down payment benefit still exists. The other protections have been eliminated.

Loans guaranteed by the Veterans Administration require military service for eligibility. A *certificate of eligibility* is issued to the veteran. If you have served in the military or were activated from the National Guard, you may be eligible. Type "VA loans" into your search engine or go to **www.va.gov**, then click on "Home Loans," for complete information.

Although you can contact the VA directly to determine eligibility, the VA recommends that you first contact a lender. Most lenders now have access to a database that will enable them to determine whether you are eligible. A second reason to see a lender first is the same as for any loan that you plan to get. You can be prequalified or preapproved. You will have a good idea of the price range that is realistic for your new home. Call your local VA office for a list of lenders in your area.

It is important to note that spouses of deceased veterans may be eligible. There are also special programs for disabled veterans and direct loans to Native Americans for certain tribal lands.

In addition to the veteran status necessary to be eligible, the site provides information on using eligibility more than once, the types of properties that can be purchased, assuming a VA loan, and the various types of loans that are offered.

Any of the following reasons are acceptable as an eligible loan purpose for a VA loan:

- to buy a home;
- to buy a townhouse or condominium unit in a project that has been approved by VA;
- to build a home;
- to repair, alter, or improve a home;
- to simultaneously purchase and improve a home;
- to improve a home through installment of a solar heating and/or cooling system, or other energy efficient improvements;
- to refinance an existing home loan;
- to refinance an existing VA loan to reduce the interest rate and add energy efficient improvements;

- to buy a manufactured (mobile) home and/or lot;
- to buy and improve a lot on which to place a manufactured home that you already own and occupy; and,
- to refinance a manufactured home loan in order to acquire a lot.

> ## From the Expert
> Advantages to the VA loan are that FHA does require a minimum of 1% down, and the mortgage insurance premium is higher than the VA guaranteed cost.

The VA guaranteed loan has many of the same benefits and drawbacks as the FHA insured loan. Down payment requirements are significantly lower than conventional financing, and closing costs may be less. Even though VA loans have no maximum loan cap, they currently top out at about $240,000 because of the inability to sell higher amount mortgages in the secondary market.

You will find two charts taken from the Government National Mortgage Association (Ginnie Mae) website on the following pages. The first shows a purchase price of $200,000, with $25,000 available for a down payment. The second shows the same purchase with no money available for a down payment. You can see that only the VA loan works with no down, and then only if the seller pays all the buyer's costs.

$25,000 available for a down payment

	Loan A: FHA Regular	Loan B: VA Regular	Loan C: Conventional
Max Sale Price	$200,000	$200,000	$200,000
Loan Amount	$180,745	$189,916	$170,000
Loan Type	Fixed	Fixed	Fixed
Loan Rate/ Term	6.0/30 yr	6.0/30 yr	6.0/30 yr
Monthly Mortgage Payment	$1,448	$1,430	$1,420
Other Monthly Housing Costs	$442	$442	$442
Total Monthly Housing Cost	$1,889	$1,872	$1,862
Down Payment	$25,000	$25,000	$30,000
Closing Costs	$1,807	$7,230	$6,851
Total Cash Required at Closing	$25,000	$25,000	$36,851

$0 available for a down payment

	Loan A: FHA Regular	Loan B: VA Regular	Loan C: Conventional
Max Sale Price	$200,000	$200,000	$200,000
Loan Amount	$198,365	$204,100	$170,000
Loan Type	Fixed	Fixed	Fixed
Loan Rate / Term	6.0/30 yr	6.0/30 yr	6.0/30 yr
Monthly Mortgage Payment	$1,560	$1,515	$1,420
Other Monthly Housing Costs	$442	$442	$442
Total Monthly Housing Cost	$2,002	$1,957	$1,862
Down Payment	$6,000	$0	$30,000
Closing Costs	$1,984	$7,542	$6,851
Total Cash Required at Closing	$7,984	$7,542	$36,851

In summary, the VA loan is an excellent loan if the seller is having a problem selling the property. The requirements to qualify (except for eligibility) are more liberal than a conventional loan. No down payment and allowing the seller to pay closing costs enable the veteran to buy the property when a nonveteran would not qualify.

In a seller's market, there are buyers who qualify for conventional financing. The amount to be borrowed can be much higher and the time to closing weeks shorter. As with FHA, it can be a good loan for the buyer, if a willing seller can be found.

Chapter 14

Hard Money Mortgages

There are two definitions of a *hard money mortgage*. The first is any mortgage loan not used to purchase the mortgaged property. This definition is used for purposes of foreclosure in states that do not allow a deficiency judgment for purchasing money mortgages. This is discussed in Chapter 20,. which deals with foreclosures.

The second definition is a loan that is also referred to as a *sub-prime* or *substandard* loan. There is no exact definition of what makes a loan sub-prime or substandard. The classification of loans ranges from *A loans* (which are the best for the borrower), to *B* and *C loans* (usually having a 2%–3% higher interest rate than the highest rate A loan), to *hard money loans*. The hard money loans carry a much higher rate and higher points than B and C loans. There are variations within each category, ranging from small variations for A loans to the largest variations for hard money loans.

Bridge Loans

A common type of hard money mortgage loan is the *bridge* or *gap* loan. As the names imply, it is used to connect transactions (bridge) or fill a void between transactions (gap). The following are examples of the use of these loans.

- Your home is in foreclosure. You can sell it and come out with some money, but you need time to do this. You already have a buyer and

have opened escrow. You get a temporary loan to reinstate your mortgage until your sale is finalized.

- You want to buy property, but have to act immediately. You can either sell other property or arrange financing to cover the purchase, but you do not have time for either. You get a hard money loan until you can either sell or arrange suitable financing.

- You have a small business. You have an opportunity to buy inventory at a once-in-a-lifetime price. You know that you can make a large profit, but you need cash to take advantage of the deal. You get a hard money loan until you can sell off enough of the product to pay it off.

All of these loans involve the borrower mortgaging property—usually his or her home—for a short period of time. Most of these loans are for one year or less. They depend on equity for security, and the borrower's credit or income-to-debt ratios are of secondary importance. The loans fund quickly—some as fast as one week.

The up-front cost of these loans is usually one or two points, plus miscellaneous fees. The higher cost comes when the loan is repaid. This can be as high as 10% of the balance.

Sub-Prime Loans

The second type of hard money loan is the longer-term loan at an exceptionally high interest rate with high points and fees. The loan can be used for any purpose. It is the loan borrowers get when their credit or income problems disqualify them from getting a B or C loan.

Home Ownership and Equity Protection Act

Not surprisingly, borrowers getting these loans tend to be less educated about finances and more susceptible to what is known as *predatory lending* practices. To protect these borrowers, the federal *Home Ownership and Equity Protection Act* (HOEPA) was passed. The Act does not prohibit lenders from charging the high rates and points, but does require them to

disclose to the borrower what is being charged and the borrower's right to refuse the loan.

The Act's disclosure requirements come into play under certain conditions. The *triggers*, as they are called, happen when the Annual Percentage Rate exceeds 8% above the Constant Maturity Treasury Bill index for first mortgages, and 10% for junior mortgages. A second trigger is when points and fees exceed the greater of 8% of the loan amount, or $465 (adjusted annually).

Other provisions include prohibiting *flipping*, the practice of refinancing loans for no apparent benefit to the borrower in order to generate loan fees. The Act prohibits refinancing a HOEPA loan with another HOEPA loan within one year, unless it is in the *best interest of the borrower*.

Another significant requirement is that the lender must consider the borrower's ability to repay the loan rather than basing the loan entirely on the equity in the property. Many loans were made knowing that there was little chance the borrower could make the required payments. As long as the property could be sold at the foreclosure auction for enough to repay the loan, the loan was made.

There are also restrictions on balloon payments for loans of less than five years and a prohibition of *arbitrary calls*. This prevents the lender from demanding that you repay the loan in full, even if you have been making your payments as agreed and are not selling the property. The practice of calling the loan was used to force the borrower into an expensive refinance.

Some states have enacted laws that extend beyond HOEPA. The most significant are those that take away the *holder in due course* protection from secondary lenders. The buyer of a loan in the secondary market is protected from liability even if the original lender unfairly took advantage of the borrower, unless the secondary lender was aware of the practice. Some states now say that the secondary lender has the same potential liability as the originating lender. If you believe you were cheated by your original lender and your loan has been sold, consult an attorney. If there was fraud involved with the possibility of punitive damages, some lawyers will take the case on a contingency fee basis.

> **From the Expert**
>
> One side benefit of HOEPA is that some lenders lowered rates and fees to avoid having their loans covered by the Act.

The argument against restrictions of hard money mortgages is that they take away the ability to borrow from those who need the money most. In order to prevent this, laws like HOEPA are designed to cover only the most egregious practices. A Federal Reserve study estimates that only about 5% of hard money loans fall under the protection of HOEPA.

Predatory Lending

The reason predatory lending has risen so dramatically is that many lenders operating in the A market have subsidiary companies making hard money mortgage loans. This has made a huge amount of money available for these loans, as well as aggressive and widespread marketing. The bigger lending institutions got into the hard money business for two reasons. First, these loans are much more profitable than A loans. Second, the fast-rising cost of homes over the last several years has made these formally high-risk loans low-risk situations. Foreclosed property that did not bring enough to cover the balance owed has been a rarity in many areas of the country.

If you have been solicited by a lender to get a mortgage loan, there are certain warning signs that may indicate predatory lending.

- Is the lender insisting that you pay off your current first loan and replace it with a higher interest loan rather than getting a second mortgage for only the amount that you want to borrow?
- Is the lender insisting that you obtain credit life insurance that will pay off the loan if you die or are disabled? These are almost always bad deals. If you do decide you want this insurance, term insurance purchased through a reputable insurance company or agent will accomplish the same goal with a lower premium.
- Will the loan consolidate bills that, by some careful budgeting, you could pay off without further borrowing? Remember that paying off short-term debt by creating long-term debt should be a last resort.

Check with a local nonprofit credit counseling agency. You may not be as bad off as you have been led to believe.

- Are there inconsistencies between what you are told and what you get in writing? You may be told, for example, that you are borrowing $5000, but the paperwork shows that you are borrowing $7000 when fees are included. This practice of *packing* a mortgage loan is common with predatory lenders. You do not have to agree to take the loan unless you agree after the necessary information is disclosed. If you are told that it is too late to back out now, do not sign anything and tell the lender that you are going to check with a lawyer before going any further.

- Get all promises in writing. Refusing to give you in writing what the terms of your loan will be is a warning sign. Predatory lenders want to give you all the bad news as late as possible. If they can wait until you are truly desperate for the money, there is a better chance you will agree to almost anything.

Most predatory lending is avoided by shopping around. If you start with your local bank, savings and loan, and credit union, you should get a pretty good idea as to where you fit as a borrower. If your only hope is a hard money loan, be sure there is no way you can do without the money. If you still want the loan, talk to two or three mortgage loan brokers to try to find the best terms available for you.

Finally, allow yourself as much time as possible. If you know that you are probably going to need to borrow money six months from now, do not wait five months before exploring your options. The major reason people agree to bad loans is that they need the money immediately.

Chapter 15

Junior Loans

A junior mortgage is one that is subordinate to at least one other mortgage. A common example would be a home improvement loan.

Example: You want to put a swimming pool in your yard, but you have a good rate on your mortgage and do not want to refinance. Instead, you borrow money to build the pool and give a second mortgage to the lender. This second mortgage is called a junior mortgage, also called a junior lien.

There is no limit to the number of mortgages you can give. There can be a third, fourth, fifth, and so on, mortgage. However, once you pass two or three, it is unlikely that you are going to be able to find a lender willing to take a fourth or fifth.

The reason the junior mortgage is sometimes less desirable to the lender is that there is an order of payment in the event of foreclosure. A first mortgage has priority. If it is foreclosed upon, the proceeds from the sale will go to the first mortgagee to pay the loan balance (plus costs of foreclosure). If there is money left over, it will go toward what is owed on the second mortgage. If there is still money available, it will pay the third mortgage. If, after all mortgagees have been paid, there is still money available, it goes to the owner of the property. The buyer at the foreclosure takes the property free of all mortgages.

From the Expert

The amount of the mortgage has nothing to do with priority. There can be a first mortgage for $10,000 and a second for $100,000. If you owe a relatively small amount of money on a low-interest first mortgage, you should weigh the costs of a second, compared to refinancing, even if you want to borrow more than the balance on the first.

If a second mortgage is foreclosed upon, it has no effect on the first mortgage. The buyer at the foreclosure sale will have to keep the first mortgage current or pay it off in order to keep the property. The buyer will take the property free of any mortgages junior to the second, such as a third or forth. The lower the position of the mortgage, the less chance there will be enough equity in the property to pay it off.

A holder of a junior mortgage can stop the foreclosure of a superior mortgage by making up the delinquent amount and adding it to his or her mortgage. He or she can then begin foreclosure of his or her mortgage if the mortgagor does not pay the delinquency.

How a mortgage is classified as first, second, etc., is strictly based on when the mortgage was dated and recorded. Unless there is mistake or fraud involved, the process is simple. A mortgage is dated when it is signed and then recorded in the county where the property is located. Recording gives what is called *constructive notice*. This means that a subsequent mortgagee, for example, would legally know of this mortgage — even if he or she had no actual knowledge of it.

Different states follow different rules for priorities and notice. In fact, there are three different theories as to priorities and notice, depending on the jurisdiction. If a borrower gives simultaneous mortgages to several lenders in order to defraud them, or if a lender fails to record the mortgage, these theories become very important. For the purposes of this discussion, there is no reason to detail them further.

Since a junior mortgage is considered less secure than a first mortgage, you will pay more in points and fees. It is a good idea to compare the benefits of a second mortgage over refinancing your first mortgage. Sit down with the real estate specialist at your bank and get the cost of each.

As with all mortgages, shop around. Start with banks and credit unions. If the loan is for a home improvement, both FHA and VA offer insurance and guarantees for these loans. You may even borrow an amount that exceeds the current value of your home in certain instances.

The Piggyback Loan

An increasingly common junior loan is the *piggyback loan*. On conforming loans, lenders are required to have the borrower obtain private mortgage insurance on loans over an 80% loan-to-value ratio. The cost of the insurance is not paid to the lender. The piggyback loan allows the lender to make more money and the borrower, in most cases, to pay less.

> **From the Expert**
> There may be other liens against a mortgaged property, such as judgments or IRS tax liens. These may be superior to, or inferior to, any mortgages. If you have judgments or tax liens against you, and you are planning to refinance or get a second mortgage loan, you may be required to pay them off.

The lender offers the borrower two loans. The first mortgage is for 80% loan to value. This does not require private mortgage insurance. A second loan of 5% to 20% is *piggybacked* to the first mortgage to create a mortgage package that allows the borrower to buy the property with less than 20% down, sometimes all the way to 0% down. The second loan is at a higher rate than the first, but usually less than what the borrower would pay for a first, at over 80% with private mortgage insurance. The lender makes money by charging the higher rate on the second loan, in effect becoming the private mortgage insurer.

The other savings to the borrower is that the interest on the piggyback is tax deductible, whereas private mortgage insurance is not. If you are in a situation in which you want to finance more than 80% of the purchase price, ask your potential lender about it. Then, calculate the higher interest rate of the piggyback against the cost of private mortgage insurance. Remember that private mortgage insurance is dropped once you have paid the loan down to under 80% of the loan to value. The higher interest on the piggyback will last for the life of the loan. If you are not sure about

your calculations, check with your accountant or simply ask your lender or mortgage broker to figure it out for you.

Another advantage to the piggyback is that it is for a small amount—somewhere from 5% to 20% of your combined loans. This means that by making relatively small additional principal payments, you can pay it off quickly.

> **Example:** Compare two loans with a 10% cash down payment. One is a 90% with PMI. The other is a 80% loan with a piggyback loan for another 10%. With the first loan, you have to pay the loan down to 80% before you can get rid of the PMI portion of the payment. While paying PMI, no portion of that payment goes toward reducing your principal balance and it is not deductible from your taxes.
>
> With the second loan, there is no PMI and every payment goes toward reducing your principal balance. If the PMI portion of the payment for the first loan is the same amount as the payment for the piggyback loan, you will have your total outstanding mortgage balance down to 80% much faster.

In most cases, the amount you have to pay each month on the piggyback loan will be less than the amount you would have to pay in PMI. If you take the savings and make additional principal payments on your remaining mortgage, you can substantially reduce the term and the amount of interest over the life of the loan. (Prepayment penalties could ruin this plan, which is why you should always ask about them.)

The piggyback is also useful if you have other assets that you want to keep. If you own high interest bonds or stock that you really believe will go up, you do not want to sell these assets to come up with 20% down for your home purchase. You may want to get the piggyback loan until the stock goes up. Then, you can sell the stock and pay off the loan. Be sure to find out in advance what it will cost both to get the piggyback and to pay it off. You can then figure out how much your stock will have to go up to make it worthwhile. Your accountant's advice may help you make the right decision.

The SingleFile Mortgage

Although the *SingleFile mortgage* is not a junior loan, it is included in this chapter because it is an alternative to getting a junior loan (piggyback) in order to avoid PMI. It is offered to lenders by Mortgage Guarantee Insurance Corporation of Milwaukee, Wisconsin (MGIC), America's largest volume home mortgage insurer. If it interests you, find a lender that offers it. Check the usual places—banks, credit unions, and mortgage brokers. Also, read the information available from MGIC's website at **www.mgic.com/singlefile.html**.

The SingleFile is a lender-paid PMI. MGIC calls it *lender-paid mortgage insurance* (LPMI). The lender, instead of the borrower, pays the mortgage insurance premium, and then charges the borrower higher interest to make up the cost.

It is unclear at this time, even to MGIC, how much information must be disclosed to the borrower under the *Home Ownership and Equity Protection Act.* (see Chapter 14.) Because of this, you have to ask the right questions. You want to compare the cost to the lower interest rate with PMI, as well as the cost compared to the piggyback. There is not the same policy of the refund once the loan gets to 80% or 78%. See if there is the possibility of an interest rate decrease after the loan is paid down. There are several LPMIs, not just the SingleFile. Ask which your lender is using. There is no refund on the SingleFile as there would be if PMI were paid up-front by the borrower, or payment reduction as there would be if PMI were financed.

An added cost to this mortgage is the amount of insurance that your lender requires. On a 100% loan, your lender can buy insurance to cover 20%, 25%, 30%, or 35% of the loan amount. Depending on your loan-to-value ratio and the length of your term, the difference can be over half a point. A lender requiring 20% coverage does not have to charge you as much interest as a lender requiring 35% coverage.

The loan targets borrowers with little cash, good credit, and good income-to-debt ratios. Since many borrowers with little cash often do not have the other two requirements, it is not for everyone. You must have a

minimum FICO score of 700–720 for some LPMI programs—and an income-to-debt ratio of no more than 45%. This means that your debts, including your new mortgage debt, are not more than 45% of your gross income.

Under this program, a borrower can pay less than 20% down—all the way to zero down. As discussed above, the required private mortgage insurance is paid as additional interest, rather than separately. The advantage is that this payment is now tax deductible. Private mortgage insurance paid separately is not.

The program is offered to compete with the piggyback loan and can save you money in some cases. For example, if you intend to pay off the piggyback in a year or two, you are better off with the piggyback. You avoid private mortgage insurance and the higher interest on the piggyback will only last for the short period. If you are going to simply make the required minimum payments on any loan you get, the SingleFile can save you more money with a lower interest rate than with the piggyback.

As usual, it is not clear which loan is best for you unless you can accurately predict your financial future. As with any loans you are comparing, check the cost of getting the loan (points and fees), the cost over the life of the loan (interest rate), and the cost of paying off the loan (fees and prepayment penalties).

There are other loans with no down payment. You can get a 100% loan and even finance your closing costs up to 3% of the loan amount. Your interest rate will be higher than if you pay your own closing costs.

As discussed above, the 80/20 piggyback loan has one major advantage over the SingleFile as it can be used to reduce your payment. You can take a 30-year first loan for 80% and a ten-year second for 20%. After ten years, the 20% loan is paid off, and the next twenty years require a payment based on only 80% of the amount that you originally borrowed. If you used the 100% SingleFile loan, you would make your payment for thirty years based on 100% of the amount originally borrowed.

Both of these loan programs offer fixed-interest rates.

Chapter 16

Home Equity Loans

Home equity loans are loans that are not used to purchase property. The loan is secured by property that you already own. The loan can be secured by a first mortgage, but it is usually secured by a second mortgage.

The equity in your home is the difference between its value and what you owe on it. For example, if your home has a value of $300,000, and you have a first mortgage of $100,000, your equity is $200,000.

You can get a home equity loan for any reason, but the reason may determine how much you get and how much you pay for it. The following are four examples of reasons you may want this loan.

1. You get a loan in order to add a room to your home. The room addition will increase your home's value. For this reason, you can get a loan of up to 125% of the current value of your home. These loans are available as FHA, VA, or conventional loans from banks and credit unions.

2. The purpose of the loan is for your child's college tuition. There is financing available specifically for this purpose. You may be able to get a lower-than-usual interest rate.

3. You want to pay off existing debt, such as high interest credit cards. Because paying off this debt will give you a higher credit score, your interest rate and fees may be slightly lower than if you are borrowing to increase your debt. These are risky loans if you run up your credit cards again. If you do not have the discipline to start using your credit cards wisely, this is a bad loan.

4. You are borrowing money to travel or make a purchase, such as furniture. You are simply creating debt. This is usually a bad reason to
borrow. Once the trip is over or the furniture starts looking shabby
or outdated, you are still going to be paying on the mortgage. You
will not get any break on interest rates or fees for this loan.

As with any loan, your credit and debt ratios will be a factor in determining interest rates and fees. Another factor will be the real estate market.

When home prices are rising and interest rates are falling, lenders are
understandably anxious to make mortgage loans. Because they feel that
the risk is low, they may offer loans that have a much higher loan-to-value
ratio, such as 90%, 95%, or even 100%. However, it serves as a word of
caution to remember that in the late 1970s and early 1980s, the market was
very different. It was not uncommon to have rates as high as 15% to 20%
for mortgage loans. Further, even those who could afford the mortgage
found it difficult to get approved.

Lenders set their own policies. When home prices are falling and interest
rates are rising, lenders not only want higher rates and fees, they want
higher credit scores and lower debt ratios.

Home Equity Line of Credit

An equity line of credit can be the best or worst of loans. The qualification
is for a maximum amount of money that can be borrowed. The borrower
can then write a check for any amount up to the maximum. No interest is
paid until money is borrowed, and then only on the amount borrowed.

The benefit to this type of loan occurs when you are not sure how
much money you will need. For example, you have a small business.
From time to time, you have the opportunity to buy products at greatly
reduced prices from distress sales. You have to act immediately when the
opportunity presents itself, but you do not know how much money you
will need for any given purchase.

If you borrow money and wait for the opportunity to arise, you will
pay interest on the amount you have borrowed. When the opportunity
finally comes along, you may need much less than you borrowed. If

you apply for a loan when the opportunity arises, it may pass before the loan goes through.

Another good use of the loan is purchasing another property. You can take advantage of distress sales by offering to purchase the property immediately. Other buyers may have to make offers subject to getting a loan. You are, in effect, a cash buyer. You can almost always get a better deal when you buy this way. Investors usually have a line of credit available. When they come across a profitable venture and the seller needs the cash right away, they are in a position to act.

> **From the Expert**
>
> A line of credit gives you the advantage of having money available interest free, and only borrowing the exact amount you need when you need it.

These are examples of the best use of the credit line. Unfortunately, many borrowers use the credit line to their disadvantage. Instead of using the credit line to make money, they use it to create debt. Furniture, automobiles, travel, borrowing by relatives, and so on can all be financed with the credit line.

You have to take a realistic view of your monetary discipline. One way to do this is to look at your credit card use. Go over your purchases for the past few years. Are there lots of impulse buys that you now regret? Are you making minimum payments or not bringing down your balance because there is always something you want? If so, stay away from a credit line. If you cannot handle a credit card with a ten or twenty thousand dollar limit, imagine the trouble you will get into with a hundred or two hundred thousand dollar limit.

How It Works

The way an equity line of credit works is simple. You apply for a loan in the normal manner. You put up real estate as *collateral security* (give a mortgage on your home). Once you are approved, you have access to any or all of the money up to the loan limit.

Your interest rate will be adjustable, unless the term is short. You will not be offered a fixed rate on a 30-year loan, for example, since you could

simply wait for rates to go up and then borrow at the fixed lower rate.

Some lenders allow you to convert to a fixed-rate loan once the line has been used. If you wrote a check against your adjustable rate line of credit for $100,000, you could convert that amount to a fixed-rate loan. Since you have already qualified, there are usually no or small fees charged. This would be beneficial if you wrote the check expecting to repay the loan quickly and now must keep it for a longer time.

Not only will your interest rate be adjustable, the cap (maximum interest rate) will most likely be very high, especially if the term is twenty or thirty years. Most adjustable loans will have a cap of about 5%. If you borrow at 5% interest, for example, you will never have to pay more than 10%, regardless of the market interest rate. With a line of credit, your cap on a 5% loan could be 15% percent or more, bringing the highest rate you could pay to 20% percent or higher.

The reason that the line of credit has a higher cap is because it is *revolving*. This means that you can borrow, pay back, and then borrow again. This will go on for the life of the loan, which could be as long as thirty years. It is really a credit card with your home used as security. The difference is in the amount. A credit card will usually have a maximum amount that can be borrowed in the thousands, sometimes tens of thousands for strong borrowers. The equity line of credit can be in the hundreds of thousands. It is easy to see the financial difficulty an equity line of credit can create.

Example: You owe $10,000 on your credit card at 10% interest. Your interest amount is $1000 per year. Interest rates rise to 20%, as they did in the 1980s. Your interest amount is now $2000 per year. With some wise budgeting, you can probably pay the interest plus something on the principal. In a few years you can pay off the debt.

You owe $200,000 on an equity line of credit at 5%. Your yearly interest is $10,000. Interest rates go to 20%. Your yearly interest is

now $40,000. Even with careful budgeting, most borrowers have difficulty making the interest payment, let alone reducing the principal.

The problem is that you do not need to be wealthy to get an equity line in the six figure range. Anyone with good credit and an ordinary job can get that much or more if there is sufficient equity in the home.

Once interest rates rise substantially, there are other problems. High interest usually means falling property prices. In those situations, the equity you borrowed against may shrink, and it may be more difficult to sell or refinance the property to pay back the loan. If the debt becomes unmanageable and you cannot sell the property to pay it off, you are left in foreclosure or bankruptcy.

Getting the Loan

As indicated, there are some very positive short-term uses for the money. If you decide that an equity line of credit is right for you, you will pay a fee to get the loan. This can range from a few hundred dollars and up. You will also have to pay an annual fee, just as with some credit cards. This should be under $100. As with all mortgages, the better your credit, the lower your debt ratios, and the lower the loan-to-value, the lower the fees. The term of the loan can be as long as thirty years, and the payment can be anything from interest-only to payment of both interest and principal (amortized). It will usually be interest-only, comparable to your minimum payment on a credit card. You can, of course, pay more than the required amount. As with any mortgage loan, shop around. Start with your bank and credit union. Get quotes from a mortgage broker.

Be sure the loan suits your purpose. Will you pay it off in a short time when the investment is sold? If so, the interest rate may not be too important and paying interest-only may be the way to go. Look for the lowest fees and be sure there is not a prepayment penalty. A reputable lender will not impose any prepayment penalty.

If you already have an equity line, have run up high debt, and believe interest rates are going up, do not wait. Refinance or convert as quickly as possible. You will initially have to pay a higher interest rate on your new

loan, but you will have a definite payment amount for the future. Even if you have to get an adjustable loan, it will have a reasonable cap.

A line of credit can be used to save or even make money. The following is a complex example that will not apply to most readers.

Example: You have a single family rental property that you have depreciated, or for some other reason, would like to *exchange*. A property exchange is a way of selling and buying real estate without paying tax on the profit from the sale.

Under the usual method of making an exchange, using Section 1031 of the Internal Revenue Code, you would sell your property (called the *relinquished property)* and then buy another (called *the replacement property*). There is a definite procedure for this in order to qualify—consult your tax advisor before attempting it.

Under IRS rules, you can buy the replacement property before you sell the relinquished property. You then have six months to sell the relinquished property. This is called a *reverse exchange*. The procedure is more complicated and more costly. However, more real estate and tax professionals are becoming competent to guide you through it. Some title companies have exchange departments that handle it.

Getting a line of credit allows you to find a suitable property and get a good deal as a cash buyer. You do not have to disturb the tenant in your rental until you are sure that you have a replacement property. The combination of the cash buyer advantage and not losing a tenant can be worth thousands of dollars.

The financial procedure is simple. Use your credit line to buy the new property. You then have six months to sell your current rental property. Use the money from the sale to pay off the loan from your credit line. The IRS rules are much more complicated.

Chapter 17

Refinancing

There are two parts to any refinancing of your existing mortgage. The first is whether to do it. The second is how to do it.

Whether to Do It

There are many reasons to refinance. The best reason, of course, is that it will save you money. To determine this, you have to consider the difference in the new interest rate compared to your current rate, the cost of the refinance, and how much time it will take to recoup that cost.

> **Example:** You have a $100,000 mortgage balance with an interest rate of 8%. Your monthly payment on the loan is slightly under $735. If you refinanced to obtain a 7% loan, your payment would fall to slightly over $665. You will save $70 each month. Once you know the refinancing costs, it is easy to calculate how many months it will take to come out ahead. Just divide the monthly saving into the costs. Using easy numbers, if refinance costs are $700, it would take you ten months to cover the costs. On the eleventh month, you would be ahead.
>
> Unfortunately, it is not quite that simple. If you do not pay the refinancing costs out-of-pocket, your new loan will be $100,700. This will raise your monthly payment to $670. If you pay the costs out of pocket, you lose the interest you could receive on the $700 by putting it into a savings account. These are usually small amounts

that will not affect the refinance calculations. However, if large amounts of money are involved, the importance of these factors increases greatly. If there is only a small savings by refinancing, you must consider all of the costs and savings.

How to Do It

Once you have decided to refinance, how should you go about it? Refinancing costs vary widely, usually depending on the worthiness of the borrower and the policies of the lender. As with any loan, shop around. Banks, credit unions, and mortgage brokers are all anxious to help. Typing the word "refinance" into any search engine will give you access to free calculators, as well as lenders willing to quote interest rates and costs online.

Many of the online sites will require you to give them personal information before letting you use the calculator. One that does not is called the Mortgage Research Center, at **www.mortgageresearchcenter.com**.

Another component of the refinance equation that can vary from lender to lender is the interest rate.

Example: A lender may offer a rate of 7% with almost no cost, or a 6.5% rate with a one-point fee plus closing costs. Now the variable of how long you intend to keep the loan becomes very important. The .5% reduction would save you another $30 each month. But if the point and closing costs are $1500, it will take fifty months to recoup the money ($1500 ÷ $30). If you finance the costs, add another five months. If you plan to keep the loan for ten years or only one year, the decision is easy, as there is a clear cost saving based on time for each loan. If you are in the five-year range, it is more difficult to make the decision.

Another variable to consider is whether interest rates are high or low. If rates are at historical highs, chances are they are going to fall. You may

want to refinance again within a short time. You will not have time to get back the cost of your current loan.

You also have to determine the cost of getting out of the loan. The obvious mortgage to avoid if you may want to pay it off in just a few years, either by selling or refinancing, is one with a prepayment penalty. There are less obvious costs to consider. When you pay off a mortgage loan, there are fees involved. These fees will vary depending on your location, but can amount to a few hundred dollars.

> ### **From the Expert**
> Everyone wants to tell you the cost of getting in. Few lenders tell you the cost of getting out.

When you are doing your calculations to determine how long you have to keep the loan to recoup costs, these costs should also be part of your equation. Ask the lender to give you a breakdown of what it will cost to pay off the loan. Be sure you are given all the costs and not just the lender's costs. In some areas, there may be trustee's fees, escrow fees, and title charges.

As a general rule, if you plan to keep your loan for five years or more, you can almost always find a deal in which the lower interest rate will justify the additional up-front cost. If you plan to keep the loan fewer than three years, the opposite is true. Between three and five years you have to do the calculations for your specific loan. There usually will not be too much of a difference. Since no one can reliably predict tomorrow (no less three to five years from now), you can only make an educated guess.

Other Considerations

There are other possibilities you may want to consider. A 30-year loan at 7% has a monthly payment only $10 less each month than a 25-year loan at 6.5%. At 6%, the monthly payment is $20 less. If you are not struggling with your current payment, you may want to refinance to both a lower interest rate and shorter term. The advantages are that you will save a lot of money by paying off your loan sooner, and especially with fixed-rate loans, the shorter term will usually come with a lower interest rate.

Beware of the opposite as well. Say you have twenty years left on your current loan and refinance to a 30-year loan. Even at the lower rate, you will pay more in the long run. Again, ask yourself how long you intend to keep the loan. How much would the payment be on a new 20-year loan with the lower interest rate?

If refinancing is done for the right reason, regardless of which way you decide to do it, you will save money — as long as you shop around and do your calculations. Refinancing to pull money (equity) out of your home to incur more debt is not a good idea.

Example: You refinance your $100,000 loan with a $150,000 loan to get $50,000 cash. You buy a car, some furniture, and take a trip. You now have to pay back $150,000 and increase the risk of losing your home.

Refinancing to reduce debt is a good idea. Think long and hard before refinancing to create debt.

Chapter 18

Manufactured Housing

Because of its lower cost compared to traditionally built homes, called *stick built* homes, the manufactured home is popular in many areas of the country. This is especially true in areas that have low land costs.

There is a common misconception that any home that has its components built in a factory is a manufactured home. There are three types of homes that have much of their construction done in a factory. They are the manufactured home (formerly called a mobile home), a modular home, and a panelized home.

The difference is that the manufactured home is almost entirely built and assembled at the factory, then installed at the site. The modular and panelized homes have their components built in the factory, but are assembled at the site.

Another major difference is that the modular and panelized homes are controlled by local building codes. The manufactured home falls under the federal *Manufactured Home Construction and Safety Standards* (MHCSS). These are *Department of Housing and Urban Development* (HUD) rules that went into effect on June 15, 1976. Factory-built homes constructed before that time are called mobile homes.

The HUD rules completely cover the building of the manufactured home, including requirements such as how strong of a wind it will withstand and how much weight the roof will hold. HUD works with state agencies to inspect both factories and their products. Each manufactured home has a certification label and data plate naming its manufacturer and

contact information, as well as technical data. For example, the plate could state that the home cannot withstand high winds and should not be located within a certain distance from a coast.

When mortgage financing is involved, there are two factors to make the home eligible. First, it must meet the HUD manufacturing standards, and second, it must be a permanently installed structure.

Manufactured homes qualify for FHA and VA loans, as well as RHS loans—those made by the Rural Housing Service of the Department of Agriculture. Mortgages on manufactured homes can also be sold to Fannie Mae and Freddie Mac.

The requirements for a manufactured home to be eligible for a mortgage Freddie Mac will buy are typical of those required by lenders in general. However, it considers mortgages on manufactured homes to have a higher risk than other homes. For this reason, it does not buy all the mortgages that it would from traditionally built homes.

Finding the right mortgage for a manufactured home can be a little more difficult. The best way to get mortgage financing for a manufactured home is to talk with local lenders that are established in the area. In many instances, smaller local banks are better than major banks. This is because the major banks may have policies that are set by people far from your town. These executives may not be located in an area where manufactured homes are common and may know little about them.

Just as Freddie Mac says that mortgages on manufactured homes are considered a higher risk loan, originating lenders will also require a premium in most instances. Expect to pay a higher interest rate than charged for mortgages for traditionally built homes in the same area.

Good information is also available from the HUD website at **www.hud.gov**. Specific information for government loans can be found on the websites of FHA, VA, and RHS. To locate these sites, just type the initials into a search engine.

By typing "manufactured housing loans" into your search engine, you will find thousands of websites dealing with and offering mortgages and rate quotes. You will easily find the range of interest rates and costs in your area.

Chapter 19

Inflation

The current Federal Reserve Board — the group who sets interest rates — has a history of worrying much more about inflation than recession. They will not hesitate to raise rates quickly if they believe inflation is on the way. It is worth noting the detrimental effect of inflation on mortgages and the real estate market in general.

There are two basic reasons for inflation. The good reason is that the economy is booming. Companies are expanding and competing for workers by offering higher salaries. The jobless rate is very low. Since more people are working for high wages, they buy more things, such as cars, appliances, and clothes. This higher demand causes higher prices (inflation). To keep the inflation rate under control, interest rates are increased. This causes less expansion and spending, lowering the demand for both workers and products.

The other reason for inflation (the bad reason) is when the economy is slow, but prices are rising. Oil prices, for example, may be high. If oil prices stay high for a sustained period, it costs more for companies to produce products and offer services. This results in lower profits, and eventually, losses. The companies first try to increase productivity by closing unprofitable factories, retail stores, etc., which causes layoffs. They also reduce workers' benefits and attempt to negotiate pay cuts with unions. Once it is no longer possible to fight the rising costs by increased productivity, they pass the increased costs on to the consumer. Since there are fewer jobs and lower wages, there is less demand for products and services.

Even though demand is lessened, prices do not fall because of the higher production costs. Interest rates go up to further add to the problem. The result is a lower standard of living until a solution is found to resolve what is keeping production costs—and thus, prices—high.

Inflation and Mortgages

What does this have to do with mortgages? If you want to sell your home, you need a buyer. When interest rates are low, more potential buyers qualify for mortgage loans. The low interest rates mean low monthly payments. Every time there is an interest rate increase, a number of buyers no longer qualify. Others now qualify only for lower loan amounts. Unlike a business, you cannot increase productivity. The only thing you can do to sell is to reduce your asking price.

> **Example:** If your home is worth $200,000 with interest rates at 5%, it may only sell for $150,000 if rates go to 8%. If you still owe $180,000, you can see the problem that you face.

Fortunately, real estate is called a *self-correcting asset*. If you bought Enron stock for $100 per share, you have lost your money no matter how long you hold the worthless shares. If you paid $200,000 for your home and it is now worth $150,000, do not worry—if you hold it long enough, it will be worth $250,000. That is a pretty sure bet. The question of how long you will have to hold it is the unpredictable part.

As discussed throughout this book, many of the decisions regarding mortgages should be based on how long you keep the loan. How long you plan to stay in your home should be decided before you start your mortgage shopping. Only about 5% of 30-year mortgages are paid off in thirty years. Since you cannot depend on favorable interest rates for refinancing, your plan should be based on how long you plan to stay in your home before selling. Then you get the loan best suited to your five-, ten-, fifteen-, or twenty-year (or longer) plan.

Chapter 20

Foreclosure

Foreclosure is the process the lender uses to take your home away if you do not make your payments. The lender can foreclose for other reasons, but nonpayment is the overwhelming reason (and the only one discussed in this book).

There are two types of foreclosure. *Judicial foreclosure* is a court action. It is seldom used compared to what is commonly called *nonjudicial foreclosure*.

Although judicial foreclosure has its place and can be successfully used to obtain deficiency judgments when nonjudicial foreclosure cannot, you as a borrower will most likely never be faced with it. This chapter is concerned with nonjudicial foreclosure.

How Foreclosure Works

The process of foreclosure is set by state and federal law, and differs depending on the location of the property (state) and type of loan. There are three steps common to every foreclosure.

First, a *notice* is given to the borrower that the loan is in *default* and that the lender intends to begin foreclosure proceedings. This notice can be given as soon as the first payment is missed or may not be sent until after several payments are missed. The foreclosure process does not begin until after the notice of default is given to the buyer, regardless of how few or how many payments have been missed.

Second, there is a period of time during which the borrower can bring the payments current, or in some other way satisfy the lender. Satisfying

the lender can be accomplished by arranging a change in the require-ments of the loan, refinancing and paying off the foreclosing lender, or selling the property and paying off the foreclosing lender. This time period will also vary depending on the location of the property and type of loan.

Third is the sale of the property at a public auction to satisfy the debt. Some states allow a period after the sale for the borrower to redeem the property. This can be as short as three days or as long as nine months. Most buyers do not redeem.

Avoiding Foreclosure

Most advice given by those who write about avoiding foreclosure says that you should find out the lender's position and policies as soon as you know that you are going to have a problem making your required pay-ment. This is not necessarily true.

When you apply for a loan, you are the boss. The lender or mortgage broker will try to accommodate you by answering any questions that you may have. That is the time to ask about foreclosure policies. If the loan is to be sold—as most are—ask to whom it will be sold and ask about their foreclosure policies.

You may feel uncomfortable asking these questions when applying for a loan, but you should not. If the person you are dealing with asks why you want to know, say that while you plan to make the payments, you like to be thor-ough and cover the negatives as well as the positives. (Or, you can say you read a book on mortgages and that was the advice in the book.)

> ### From the Expert
> Find out about the lender's foreclosure policy before taking the loan, not when you are in financial trouble and have no bargaining power.

When you ask about the lender's policy regarding foreclosure, you are not asking a general question. There are specific ways to avoid foreclosure.

There are several reasons why a borrower may have problems making the mortgage payment. Some are temporary, such as a job loss or a

temporary health problem requiring time off from work that could last for a few months. A salesperson working on commission could have this problem. The word *temporary* in the mortgage industry usually means no more than six months.

The other situation is the permanent inability to make the payments. This could be a job loss followed by a new job that pays much less, a severe health problem restricting the borrower's ability to work, or divorce.

Temporary Solutions

If the situation is temporary, the solution is usually some type of *forbearance* by the lender. This could be requiring no payments or reduced payments for a few months. This would be coupled with a repayment plan. Once the borrower is again able to pay, the repayment plan would require higher payments to make up the delinquency.

If you have a government loan, such as an FHA loan, check with that agency's *approved counselor*. You may be eligible for a no-interest loan from the agency to bring you current. Whenever approved counseling is available, use it. There may be local programs to help you of which you are not aware.

To find an approved counselor, go to the FHA website. They will supply you with a list of counselors in your area and how to contact each. As you will see from reading this chapter, there are several possible options. By giving a counselor a detailed explanation of your circumstances, you have a better chance of choosing the best solution.

Another option is *refinancing*. This works if you have substantial equity in your home.

> **Example:** Say your current mortgage was originally $200,000. You have paid for many years and the loan balance is now $100,000. Your monthly payment is still based on $200,000. You could refinance the $100,000 balance, including any delinquency, and have a much lower monthly payment.

> **From the Expert**
>
> A loan modification makes it easier to catch up on missed payments and keep the loan current in the future.

Before seeking another lender, talk to your present lender about a *loan modification*. A loan modification is changing your loan rather than paying off your existing loan and getting a new one. Depending on market conditions and your ability to pay in the future, the lender may reduce your interest rate, lengthen the term, or make some other change or combination of changes to reduce your payment.

Permanent Problems

If your situation is permanent, you have more serious problems and choices. If your income has been reduced for the foreseeable future, you may still be able to modify your existing loan or refinance to bring your payments to a manageable level. If your income has been reduced to a point where there is no way you can make even reduced payments in the foreseeable future, you are facing foreclosure.

If you have substantial equity, sell the property. You can probably get an equity line of credit to keep you going until you complete the sale.

If you have a financially strong buyer who wants to assume your loan, ask the lender about it even if your loan states that it is not assumable. This *workout assumption* may be acceptable to your lender rather than having the loan repaid in full and your buyer seeking financing elsewhere.

If you have little or no equity, approach your lender with one of two options. The first is called a *short sale*. The lender agrees to accept the proceeds of a sale even though it is less than you owe. This will work best if you have a buyer, but after all expenses of the sale, you will net somewhat less than you owe on the mortgage.

The reason for this type of arrangement is that it costs the lender time and money to foreclose. If the loss on the short sale is comparable to the loss the lender will suffer through foreclosure, it makes sense to accept the short sale.

The second option is called a *deed in lieu of foreclosure*. The deed in lieu is a direct method of turning over ownership to the lender without the foreclosure process. Again, the lender saves the time and expense of foreclosure.

When offering a deed in lieu, be sure that you have no obtainable equity. If a sale will net you some cash, the deed in lieu is not a good alternative.

Doing Nothing

You may be thinking that if you have no equity, why bother with these remedies? Why not just stay in the home until you are evicted? Many people do. There are two reasons why you should not.

First, it will ruin your credit. If there is any possible way to avoid foreclosure, the effort you make is worthwhile.

A second reason is what is called a *deficiency judgment*. This means that if after adding up what you owe on your loan — including the costs of the foreclosure — the sale does not fully reimburse the lender, you are personally responsible. If the home you used for collateral for the loan you took does not cover what you still owe, you are not just *off the hook*. The lender can go to court and get a judgment against you, and go after your wages and other assets.

Not all loans allow deficiency judgments. Some states do not allow them for the loan used to purchase your home, but do allow them for subsequent loans, such as the home improvement loan you got to put in the pool.

One question you should always ask when applying for a mortgage loan is whether it is a *nonrecourse loan*. A nonrecourse loan requires that the lender look only to the property for repayment. Regardless of the size of the loss the lender may suffer after foreclosure, it may not come after the borrower for reimbursement. In other words, deficiency judgments are not allowed.

Foreclosure Scams

When the notice that you are in default has been *recorded* (made public record at the courthouse or recorder of deeds office), you will most likely receive a host of contacts from people wanting to solve your problems by refinancing, helping you sell, or offering to buy your home.

Milking

There are two particular scams that are common. First is called *equity skimming,* or in less polite circles, *milking.* Someone offers to buy your home right now by giving you enough money to move and maybe a little more. You are not going to get anything otherwise, so it sounds like a good deal. You give a deed and move out. The milker then rents the property until the foreclosure sale and eviction of the tenants.

> ### From the Expert
> One of the most important things you can do is stay in the house until the foreclosure sale. You become ineligible for many of the programs designed to save you from foreclosure if you are not occupying the property.

The problem is that you are now stuck with a deficiency judgment. The amount of the deficiency judgment is also usually greater because of a lower auction sale price due to any damage done to the property by the tenants. Milkers are not particular about screening tenants.

The Phony Counseler

The single most important thing you can do when faced with the possibility of foreclosure is seek a qualified counselor. The second scam is the *phony counselor.*

People will contact you offering services to help you out of your predicament. If they are not really counselors, you will end up selling your home to a milker or will be taken advantage of in some other way.

Do not sign anything until you have talked to a knowledgeable person you can trust. Talk to your lawyer or accountant. Talk to the real estate

officer at your bank. Call the approved counselors from the FHA website, the Fannie Mae website, the Freddie Mac website, or even the MGIC website. You do not have to do all of these. One or two phone calls should get you to a qualified person.

Once you have found a good counselor, make an appointment. Then make a list of questions to ask about the possibilities of avoiding foreclosure based on the alternatives previously mentioned. When you get the advice, follow up on it immediately. This is not a time for procrastination.

Bankruptcy

Bankruptcy is controlled by both state and federal law. There are many books on the subject. This is not one of them. However, if foreclosure is imminent, it might be wise to consult a bankruptcy lawyer. There are two possible benefits to bankruptcy.

The first is that under Chapter 7, you may be able to eliminate the personal liability of a deficiency judgment—if one is permitted for your mortgage. Second, under Chapter 13, you may be able to restructure your mortgage payment to make up the back payments. In either case, you will be granted a temporary *stay*, in which the foreclosure proceedings will be halted. This can give you time to complete a pending sale or to come up with some other option to avoid the foreclosure.

Bankruptcy is not the answer for everyone and may in fact be more damaging than the foreclosure. However, it is another tool to consider, and for the right person, one that can be of great benefit.

Chapter 21

The Purchase Money Mortgage

This chapter is completely different from what you have read so far. It covers your position as both borrower and lender.

With all the programs now being offered, a person without a 20% down payment can usually still find a mortgage that fits his or her needs with PMI, LPMI, or a piggyback loan. Another possibility also exists, which is financing by the seller.

A seller may be willing to take a mortgage for some portion of the purchase price. There are many reasons why a seller may consider this. When mortgage rates were 20%, some sellers thought offering a 15% mortgage was a good investment. It was even recommended by some financial advisors for people retiring and moving to smaller, less costly homes. Another consideration is that a buyer may not have to qualify for a 20% loan from the bank. However, the seller could accept anyone he or she wanted, allowing the sale to go forward.

If you are in a situation in which seller financing is offered, remember that there are no guidelines. As long as the transaction does not violate any laws, whatever you agree to is binding. Always have a knowledgeable person review all documents before you sign anything. Be sure that you know the terms of the loan and prepayment penalties, if any.

The Seller

On the other side of the seller-financed loan is the seller, and there are things a seller should know about taking a mortgage. There are two defi-

nitions for *purchase money mortgages*. The first is any mortgage used to purchase the property. This is important, since some states do not allow deficiency judgments on purchase money mortgages. The second, and more common definition, is a mortgage given to the seller as part of the purchase price. This is the particular one discussed here.

If you are selling your home and a potential buyer asks if you will "take back paper" or "carry paper," you are being asked to take a mortgage for all or part of the purchase price. What are the ramifications? Purchase money mortgages almost always have a higher interest rate than other mortgage loans. You will probably get a better return than you could get elsewhere on your money. The reason you can charge a higher rate of interest is that you are giving a high risk loan.

A buyer is willing to pay higher interest for one of two reasons. One, he or she cannot get a loan from the usual sources, possibly because of poor credit. Two, the buyer does not have enough money for a sufficient down payment. Either reason creates risk.

Sellers having difficulty getting a buyer may be willing to accept a purchase money mortgage, especially if the potential buyer has good credit and is simply short of cash. This could easily be the situation with a first-time buyer. If you are interested in getting this type of mortgage, there are certain precautions you must take.

Down Payments

First, seller financing is almost always going to be a second mortgage that is subject to the first mortgage from the bank. The bank's loan is usually for the majority of the purchase price and stands first in line to get paid. If the buyer fails to pay on the first mortgage, the lender on it will foreclose and the seller financed mortgage will be wiped out. If the sale pays off the first mortgage balance—including all delinquencies and foreclosure costs—and there is money left over, the seller will get this money up to what is owed on the mortgage. It seldom happens.

You can bring the first mortgage current and add that amount on to your mortgage. This will put the borrower in default on your mortgage if the added money is not paid with the next regular payment after you

have informed the borrower of your actions and demanded payment. You can then begin your own foreclosure. If you foreclose, you will either be paid off at the sale or get back the property if no one bids enough to enable a payoff (usually the latter). If there was equity in the property, the owner would have sold it to avoid foreclosure.

Once you get back the property, you will be responsible for the first mortgage payment. Foreclosure of a first mortgage wipes out the second (third, forth, etc.). Foreclosure of a second does not affect the first.

There are problems that may arise.

- If the first is for a high amount, making up the delinquency may require more money than you can afford. This is especially true if the first mortgagee waited until the borrower was several months behind on the payments before starting the foreclosure process.
- The holder of the first may claim that the foreclosure triggers a due on sale clause and demand payment. Most state laws do not allow this. Check the applicable law in your state.
- Borrowers in possession of property being foreclosed upon do not take care of the property. Some deliberately damage it. If the second is for a relatively small amount, make sure the added expense to get ownership of the property is worth it.

For more detailed information on mortgage priorities, refer to Chapter 15 on junior loans.

Another precaution you can take concerns the first mortgage. Many types of loans do not allow the buyer to borrow the down payment. If the first lender finds out that the down payment was financed, it has the right to foreclose. You must be sure that the lender your buyer is using allows your purchase money mortgage.

Total Purchase Price

A seller could finance and take a mortgage for the total purchase price. Now the transaction is strictly between the seller and the buyer. There is no first mortgage lender to qualify the buyer or to be dealt with in a foreclosure. It is all up to the seller.

In some parts of the country, a seller customarily uses an attorney to facilitate the sale. If you live in a state where lawyers are used for home sales, be sure that you consult yours before signing anything obligating you to receive a mortgage as all or part of the purchase price.

If you live in a state where attorneys are not customarily used for home sales, you should consult one. Some state bar associations certify lawyers as experts in real estate transactions. Call your local bar association first. If your state bar cannot give you a qualified attorney, a recommendation from your bank or title company can usually help.

Have the attorney either draw the note and mortgage or examine the one that you plan to use. This is especially important if you plan to sell the mortgage. You must be sure that your note is a *negotiable instrument*. If not, you will have difficulty selling it. There are whole courses in law schools on negotiable instruments, but the important thing to know is that the documents must be drawn properly to be negotiable, and a buyer of the note and mortgage will want negotiability.

Also, have the borrower fill out a mortgage application, giving you the right to perform a credit check and employment background check. Get the buyer's tax returns for the past three years. Have your attorney examine all this information.

Scams

There is a common scam in these transactions—a subordination clause in the mortgage. This clause states that the buyer can borrow money after your mortgage is recorded and gives the new lender a mortgage superior to yours. In these clauses, you agree to subordinate your mortgage to this later loan. In other words, your first will become a second or your second will become a third. Since higher mortgages wipe out lower (junior) mortgages, you can see the danger.

The subordination clause can be called a scam. It is considered a strategy by some. Seminars on how to buy property with no money sometimes teach the subordination clause as a legitimate purchase method. This is why it is so commonly used. If you are asked by a prospective buyer to insert a subordination clause into the purchase money mortgage, you can

be fairly sure that this buyer intends to borrow the full value of the property with a mortgage or mortgages superior to yours. After you subordinate, you will be left with worthless paper unless the property greatly increases in value.

Subordination clauses are also used when construction is involved. This is an entirely different situation and subordinating to a construction loan may be desirable for a seller of land to a developer. It is not a good idea for a seller of an existing home.

> **From the Expert**
> Be sure that your title insurance policy protects you against forgeries, especially if you are going to be the only mortgagee.

Selling the Mortgage

If you do decide to *take back paper,* you can keep the mortgage or sell it. The secondary market works for individuals too. The difference is that you will not be selling yours to Fannie Mae. You will sell to a company or individual investor that buys purchase money mortgages.

The smart thing to do is investigate the market before agreeing to take the mortgage. Your real estate agent should have a contact that invests in these mortgages. You can find investors in the newspaper, but a personal recommendation is usually better. By doing this, you can get an idea of the discount you will have to give. The amount will depend on many factors, including rising or falling home prices. Do not expect the one or two points that apply to institutional lenders. You could have to discount your second mortgage by 50% or more. If you have the first mortgage for the majority of the purchase price, to sell it could require a 10% to 30% discount. Again, there are many factors involved and you may have to give a much lower discount.

Chapter 22

The Reverse Mortgage

So far, you have read about how important good credit and your income-to-debt ratios are to obtain a favorable mortgage. Now you can forget it. For a reverse mortgage, none of that matters. What is important is that you are 62 years old or older and that your home is free and clear of any other loans and mortgages, or at least, has a lot of equity.

A *reverse mortgage* is a completely different type of loan. If properly used, it can be the best thing to happen to many seniors since Social Security.

How It Works

Instead of obtaining a loan and paying it back by payments that begin a month after you borrow the money, you do not pay it back until you stop living in your home. You can see the obvious advantage for a retired person who needs money but would find it difficult to make payments.

Since you do not make payments, your ability to repay the loan is irrelevant. That is why credit and income are not considered in order to qualify. Another reason they are not considered is that the reverse mortgage is a nonrecourse mortgage. You are not personally responsible for repayment.

When it comes time to repay, the lender can look only to the property. If you have borrowed more than the property is worth because you have lived longer than the average person, it is not a problem. This means that your estate does not have to make up the shortfall. The beneficiaries of

your estate will not get less of your other assets because they have to repay your reverse mortgage. This is especially helpful for those who have substantial assets.

What You Can Borrow

How much you can borrow is based on three factors: life expectancy, the value of your home, and equity of your home. An easy way to look at life expectancy is to compare the reverse mortgage to a life insurance policy. Life expectancy for a reverse mortgage is figured exactly the opposite of life insurance. As you know, the older you get, the more you pay for life insurance. The insurer wants you to make enough payments on the policy to make a profit before having to pay the death benefit. The insurer does not know how long you will live, but knows that by writing thousands of policies, the average life expectancy of the insured is predictable.

With a reverse mortgage, older is better. Since the lender is paying you until you move or die, the older you are, the shorter your remaining life. The lender can pay more over your remaining years since there are fewer years remaining. Based on this, if you are not at least 62 years old, you are not eligible for a reverse mortgage. The average life expectancy is too great for people under age 62 for banks to take the risk of loaning money on a reverse mortgage. Just as Social Security eligibility is changing as people live longer, the minimum age for a reverse mortgage may change. If the age requirement is not raised as life expectancy increases, the amount that can be borrowed will have to be lowered.

The second factor is the value of your property. Just as with a standard mortgage, the loan amount will be limited by the value of the property. The loan-to-value ratio will be lower for a reverse mortgage, since your debt is increasing over time rather than decreasing as it would with a standard loan.

Your property's value may be even more important if the reverse mortgage has no limit. FHA limits the amount that you can borrow, just as it does for standard mortgages. Some lenders offer no-limit reverse mort-

gages. If your home is worth a million dollars and you want the biggest loan you can get, FHA is not for you.

The third factor is your equity. If you have $100,000 equity, you will not be able to borrow as much as you would if you had $200,000 equity. This is obvious and works the same way as a standard loan. The difference with some reverse mortgages is that the increasing value of your home is automatically considered.

Everyone knows that housing prices have increased over the years. Prices may fall temporarily, but the general trend is up. You would be hard-pressed to find a home today that is valued at less than it was ten or twenty years ago.

If you have a standard mortgage, you can refinance as the value of your home increases and borrow more money. With certain reverse mortgage loans, the increase in value is built into the loan. The amount you can borrow keeps increasing without the need for refinancing.

> **From the Expert**
>
> Although the theory for all reverse mortgages is basically the same, there are enormous differences in the types of reverse mortgages and from whom you borrow.

Home Equity Conversion Mortgage

The *Home Equity Conversion Mortgage* (HECM) is the most popular reverse mortgage. The guidelines allowing lenders to make this loan are offered by the Department of Housing and Urban Development. (It is FHA insured.) It requires the borrowers to:

- be 62 years of age or older;
- own the property;
- occupy the property as primary residence; and,
- participate in a consumer information session given by an approved HECM counselor.

These requirements need little explanation. Although the test for a primary residence is somewhat subjective, the general rule is that it is the

property you live in most of the time and consider your home. It is not your vacation home.

The main reason counseling is required is the notion, right or wrong, that seniors require more protection than other adults. An 18-year-old can get a loan without special counseling, but a 62-year-old has to be counseled.

Having said that, counseling is a benefit that should be available (even required) to the 18-year-old. The other reason seniors get counseling is that there is an organization that watches out for them. There is none for the 18-year-old. The *American Association of Retired Persons* (AARP), in cooperation with HUD, has a list of approved counselors. The counselor will explain to the borrower the different types of reverse mortgages, and which, if any, will help the borrower best achieve his or her objectives.

Counseling

Counseling may be the most important aspect of the HECM. A reverse mortgage, like any other borrowing, creates an obligation on the part of the borrower. Since the borrower's home is used for repayment, it also limits the borrower's use of this asset. Improper use of the reverse mortgage, like any other borrowing, can have a detrimental effect on the borrower's finances.

Suppose, for example, a person plans to move into a retirement community and rent his or her current home for additional income to defer the cost of the new residence. Would it be a good idea to get a reverse mortgage until the move? Unless our hypothetical borrower is desperate for cash, it is a bad choice.

Example: A borrower gets a reverse mortgage, uses $50,000 over five years, and then moves into the retirement community. The reverse mortgage is no longer on the borrower's primary residence and must be repaid. Since the borrower most likely does not have $50,000 to pay off the loan (he or she probably would not have taken the reverse mortgage if he or she did), he or she now has to refinance to a standard mortgage.

This immediately creates several problems.

- The repayment on the new loan begins one month after closing. Whatever rent the buyer hoped to use is now decreased by the amount of the mortgage payment.
- If the lender for the new loan treats the property as rental property, the amount available to the borrower will be lower, and the interest rate and fees will be higher.
- If the borrower is between tenants at some future date, the repayment of the mortgage will be an additional burden that will not be offset by rental income.
- There will be the cost of getting two loans—the reverse mortgage and later, the standard mortgage.

A counselor can explain the problems that can develop with a reverse mortgage and help the borrower alter his or her plan accordingly. If the reverse mortgage is still necessary, maybe the plan should be to sell the home when the borrower moves and purchase an annuity to help pay the costs of the retirement community. That would be one of several options. The important thing is that our borrower will be well informed and able to plan ahead with confidence.

Another reason for counseling is to focus on the person's reason for wanting the money. Is it to invest in some risky venture? Is it because a child does not want to wait for an inheritance? Is a con artist trying to steal the person's money? The first rule of borrowing is always to ask yourself if you should. This holds true for a ten dollar credit card purchase as well as a million dollar mortgage. Once you have decided that borrowing is to your benefit, the next step is to research the best way to borrow. The counselor can help with both decisions.

Criteria

The Home Equity Conversion Mortgage has certain criteria for the amount that can be borrowed, the financial requirements of the borrower, and the property requirements. The following should give you a good idea as to whether you and your property qualify.

The Amount that Can be Borrowed

The amount that can be borrowed is based on three things:

1. age of the youngest borrower;
2. current interest rate; and,
3. lesser of appraised value or the FHA insurance limit.

In order to get the loan, all owners of the property must be age 62 or older and must sign the mortgage. Since the payments will be made until all owners die, sell, or move out, the age and life expectancy of the youngest is used to determine the amount that can be borrowed.

Since a reverse mortgage, like any other loan, requires the borrower to pay interest, the interest rate will affect the total amount borrowed. Even though a reverse mortgage can have an adjustable interest rate, the current rate will determine how much can initially be borrowed.

A loan based on the appraised value does not mean that the borrower would receive that amount. It assumes that there are no liens on the property. If there are, they would have to be paid before the loan would be made. They could be paid out of the loan proceeds, leaving less to go to the borrower.

The FHA insurance limit is the maximum that can be borrowed, regardless of the value of the property. The limit changes as property values change and differs in different areas. The current limits are between just over $130,000 to just under $240,000. For Alaska, Guam, Hawaii, and the Virgin Islands, the FHA mortgage limits may be adjusted up to 150% of the ceiling.

Financial Requirements

The financial requirements for the loan include the following:

- no income or credit qualifications are required of the borrower;
- no repayment as long as the property is the *primary residence*; and,
- closing costs may be financed in the mortgage.

As discussed, only the property is used for repayment. Since the borrower is not personally responsible, there is no need to determine

whether he or she will be able to repay. This means that no one will be denied the loan or charged a higher interest rate because of bad credit, insufficient income, or excessive debt, as would happen with a standard mortgage. In fact, insufficient income to pay debts is a common reason to get a reverse mortgage loan.

Primary residence is a term without a precise meaning. Spending more than six months a year at the property is one test. Intent to occupy is another. Intent is determined by actions, such as the address used on one's driver's license, tax returns, and medical insurance forms.

Financing closing costs would decrease the amount that the borrower would receive in subsequent payments. For example, if a borrower was entitled to a $100,000 loan and financed $1000 in closing costs, only $99,000 would be left, regardless of which payment method the buyer chose to receive.

> ### From the Expert
> Since there is no restriction on one's income or assets to get a reverse mortgage loan, it is not uncommon for a borrower to have more than one house.

Property Requirements

Finally, there are also certain requirements that the property used for the reverse mortgage must meet. The property must:

- be a single family home or one to four unit home with one unit occupied by the borrower;
- be condominiums or *planned unit developments* (PUD) that are HUD-FHA approved;
- be cooperatives or manufactured homes that meet HUD guidelines; and,
- meet minimum property standards regarding condition (borrower may fund repairs in the mortgage).

Homes for up to four families are usually treated the same as single family homes for mortgage purposes. The requirement that the buyer occupy one of the units as his or her primary residence applies.

The requirement that a condominium or PUD be HUD-FHA approved applies to all FHA insured mortgages. If you could get a standard FHA insured loan on the property, then you can get a reverse mortgage. Most condominiums and PUDs will qualify.

A cooperative is a unit that is not owned exclusively by the occupant. The occupant owns stock in a company that owns the project with the *owner* having the exclusive right to occupy the unit. The way that the project was structured (the paperwork) will determine if it meets HUD guidelines.

The HUD standards to qualify a manufactured home for an FHA loan are discussed in Chapter 18.

Many older homes were simply not built to meet FHA standards. Others are in need of repair to reach the standards. The cost of making the changes to meet the minimum standards can be financed as part of the reverse mortgage. If the cost to meet the standards is a large amount, there may not be much left for the borrower.

Types of Reverse Mortgages

The types of reverse mortgages are really based on their different payment options. All of the following are allowed under the FHA Home Equity Conversion Mortgage, except in Texas, where reverse mortgages with lines of credit are not permitted. The qualification requirements for both the buyer and the property are the same for all payment options.

- *Tenure*—equal monthly payments as long as at least one borrower lives and continues to occupy the property as a principal residence. The age of the borrower (life expectancy) and equity in the property determine how much can be borrowed. The borrower receives payments until death, as long as the ownership and occupancy requirements are satisfied.

- *Term*—equal monthly payments for a fixed period of months selected. The age of the borrower and equity in the property determine the amount that can be borrowed. The borrower then decides on the amount of the payments. The higher the amount, the shorter the time over which they are paid. Once all payments are made, the

borrower does not receive any more money—but there is no repayment required as long as the borrower continues to live in the home.

- *Line of Credit*—unscheduled payments or in installments, at times and in amount of borrower's choosing, until the line of credit is exhausted. A reverse mortgage line of credit is the same as an equity line of credit, in that the borrower uses the credit without restriction until the limit is reached.
- *Modified Tenure*—combination of line of credit with monthly payments for as long as the borrower remains in the home. An example is probably the easiest explanation. The borrower qualifies for a loan of $100,000. Based on age, the monthly payment for life is $500. However, the borrower would like to be able to have a chunk of immediate cash available. The borrower opts for a line of credit for $50,000 and takes the balance ($50,000) in payments of $250 monthly.
- *Modified Term*—combination of line of credit with monthly payments for a fixed period of months selected by the borrower. This works just like modified tenure except that the amount remaining after deducting the line of credit is paid over an agreed-upon time period, rather than over the borrower's lifetime.

The type of loan can be changed if the borrower's circumstances change. Unlike the expense of a refinance, the current cost of restructuring the way the borrower receives the money is currently $20.

Distinguishing FHA with Non-FHA Loans

The two most important factors that distinguish the FHA insured reverse mortgage from other reverse mortgages are tenure borrowing (lifetime income) and the increase in the amount to be borrowed. Unlike most other reverse mortgages, the HECM increases the amount available to the borrower.

Example: If you are originally qualified to receive a mortgage amount of $100,000, that amount will increase each year. Currently, the rate of increase is just over 4.25%. You would have $104,250

available one year after the original qualification if no money was used.

If you chose a credit-line account and withdrew $4,250 at the end of each year, the original $100,000 would always be available. With other reverse mortgages, a withdrawal of $4,250 per year would simply reduce the amount available to $95,750, $91,500, $87,250, and so on.

The major disadvantage to the HECM is the amount that can be borrowed. If your home is worth much more than the FHA limit in your area, and you want to borrow the most you possibly can, you will want to investigate other reverse mortgage options. There are several companies offering reverse mortgage loans well beyond the limits of the HECM. These loans are generally more expensive and some do not allow lifetime payments.

A good place to start is the AARP website. AARP will take the information for your specific situation and give you a comparison of the costs involved in the available programs. They have nothing to sell you, so the information is unbiased.

Many major banks also have websites offering to help. There is no shortage of companies wanting to get you a reverse mortgage loan. As with any loan that you want, some shopping will give you a better idea of what is available that best suits your needs.

The Home Keeper Mortgage

The *home keeper* is the Federal National Mortgage Association (Fannie Mae) reverse mortgage offering. Fannie Mae does not make the loan, but will purchase the mortgage in the secondary market (provided the originating lender follows certain guidelines).

To qualify, you must be at least 62 years old and have a free and clear home or a low mortgage with substantial equity. The maximum amount you can borrow is generally higher than the HECM and is based on average home prices, rather than specific areas.

The interest rate on the adjustable loan uses a CD (certificate of deposit) index rather than the Treasury Bill index used by the HECM. The CD rate will move at a slower pace and will benefit the borrower if rates rise.

> **From the Expert**
>
> As with all reverse mortgages, the loan need not be repaid until the borrower dies or moves.

There is no personal liability on the part of the borrower or the borrower's estate. Only the mortgaged property can be used for repayment, unless the borrower or borrower's heirs choose to repay from other sources. In other words, if there is still equity in the home, the heirs may wish to sell the property or refinance it and pay off the reverse mortgage loan.

Like other reverse mortgage programs, loan origination, closing costs, and monthly service fees can all be financed. Counseling is also required by an approved counselor. The payment options include tenure, set term, or line of credit. The line of credit option is not available in Texas.

The big disadvantage of the home keeper is that there is no automatic increase in the amount you may borrow. Unless you choose tenure, you can borrow only up to the original amount for which you qualified. By contrast, the HECM loan amount increases each year. As discussed in the previous example, if you selected the line of credit option and qualified for a $100,000 loan under an HECM, and borrowed nothing for the first year, your maximum loan amount would rise to about $104,250. The same scenario under a home keeper would still have a loan amount after one year at $100,000.

The advantage to the home keeper is the higher initial amount you can borrow. This may provide even more financial security in certain circumstances. As the next section shows, borrowing the entire amount at closing and buying an annuity may be your best option.

Annuities

A common use for those who seek a reverse mortgage is to take the proceeds in a lump sum and use it to purchase an annuity. An *annuity* is a product you buy from an insurance company that pays you a sum of

money for an agreed-upon term or for life. It acts in the same way as a reverse mortgage that pays a monthly amount. However, an annuity may be a better financial solution.

Your goal is to get the largest monthly payment possible for the rest of your life. You are not sure how long you will want or be able to occupy your home. You are thinking that maybe in five years or so, you might want to move to an apartment or a senior care facility.

You can get a reverse mortgage tenure loan that will guarantee you monthly income for life. The problem is, you must occupy your home for life to get the benefit. If you move in five years, you will then have to repay the loan. How do you get the maximum benefit from your reverse mortgage without having to worry about repayment?

You can take the total amount of your reverse mortgage entitlement at closing and buy a lifetime annuity. With this comes two advantages. First, the annuity will sometimes pay a larger monthly amount than the tenure reverse mortgage. This achieves the first part of your goal, which was to get the highest monthly income available.

The second part of your goal was to have this income continue for your lifetime. What happens in five years when you move from your home? The money you borrowed on the reverse mortgage has to be repaid. If you sell your home to do this, you get the difference between the sale proceeds and the repayment amount. If there is nothing left or the home sells for less than what you owe, you get nothing. You also owe nothing if the home sells for less than what you owe because the reverse mortgage lender cannot look to you personally for repayment.

However, if you have taken the money and purchased an annuity, you keep getting your payments for as long as you live, regardless of where you live. You now have your monthly payment without the burden of the reverse mortgage.

From the Expert
This combination of reverse mortgage borrowing and annuity buying is ideal for some.

Choosing between an Annuity or Reverse Mortgage

The person who wants to stay in the property for a lifetime and then leave as much equity as possible to the children is better off with the tenure loan. The reason is that, by borrowing the full amount on the reverse mortgage to buy the annuity, interest will accrue on the total borrowed. The amount owed at the death of the borrower will be substantially more than if the money was taken monthly, and if it was taken all up-front, the borrower reduces the equity amount that will go to the children.

A person who wants to have cash on hand for emergencies, but does not need more monthly income, would obviously not be interested in the annuity.

NOTE: *A reminder for Texans: you cannot take all your money at closing or through a line of credit.*

Future Problems

There is a problem in reverse mortgage loans that may soon have to be addressed. An increasing number of homes being taken back by lenders after the borrower moves or dies are in poor condition. There are many theories as to the reasons, but the main one is fairly obvious. Once a borrower believes that his or her home will have no equity, the *pride of ownership* is lost. Why spend the money to make repairs or repaint? Unless there is an emergency repair needed, you are fixing up someone else's home.

Currently, it is not common for lenders to make inspections or have maintenance agreements specifically for reverse mortgage borrowers, but it may come to that. Reverse mortgages are relatively new. As the baby boomers hit age 62, there will be a dramatic increase in the number of these loans. The maintenance problem will become more serious. If you are getting a reverse mortgage loan, ask your counselor if there are any new maintenance requirements.

Reverse Mortgage Comparison Worksheet

To use the reverse mortgage worksheet, put in the type of loan, like *lifetime*, *term*, or *lump sum*. Then compare them against your objective. It may be maximum monthly payment to you without regard to equity reduction or simply the most you could borrow for emergencies without any monthly payments to you. You also want to compare your highest monthly income from the mortgage against the highest income you could receive from an annuity if you took the reverse mortgage money in a lump sum and bought an annuity for a definite term or for your lifetime.

Reverse Mortgage Comparison Worksheet

	Loan 1	Loan 2	Loan 3	Loan 4	Loan 5
Type of Loan					
Loan Amount					
Term					
Yearly Value Increase					
Interest Rate					
Monthly Payment					
Total Interest over Term					
Annuity Payment					

Chapter 23

First-Time Buyers

This chapter is written to prepare you both for your home purchase and your mortgage. If you follow the advice and use the worksheet, you should be prepared to assist both your real estate agent and your lender to get the home and mortgage that is right for you.

Budget

Most people do not really know their spending habits. The main reason for this is that they are busy and do not want to spend the time and effort necessary to keep track of every little thing they spend money on. This is especially true if they are not having financial difficulties.

The purpose of creating a budget is to see what kind of home and how much of a mortgage loan you can really afford. The reward is that most find they can afford more than they realized.

The first step in the process is to determine your income. Find your tax returns for the last three years—five would be even better. You are almost certainly going to need at least two years' returns for your lender anyway. Recent paycheck stubs will also be needed, along with W-2 statements for the past few years showing your yearly income.

If you are salaried, you look at your gross income and the changes over the years. This should show you (and your lender) if your income steadily increased, decreased, or was relatively stable. *Stable* means that it kept up with inflation. If there was no increase or an increase less than inflation over the years, it will be considered to have decreased.

Commissions

This is pretty straightforward. However, if your income is not salaried, you have to take extra steps.

> **Example:** You are a salesperson and commissions are your main source of income. Commissions are not considered as reliable as salary. This is because commissions generally correspond directly to how hard you work, rather than if you show up for work and do an adequate job. Taking a couple of weeks off due to illness, for example, could affect commission earnings much more than salary. Loss of one large account is another example of a possible problem.

If your tax returns show that your commission earnings have increased over the years, you may be in even better shape than a salaried person. Many types of commission earnings depend on residual earnings. If you sell insurance, you may get a commission for every renewal, or even every payment made on the policy. Your income this year would include not just the policies that you sold this year, but the residuals on the ones you sold last year and the year before. Examine your income from this prospective. Also, look at the negative aspect. Will a substantial amount be going down because some of your residuals will be ending shortly? Your lender may miss this, but you should be prepared for the income reduction.

The second part of your examination should cover the times during the year your commissions are earned. If you sell wrapping paper, you might make 75% of your money in the last quarter of the year. If you apply for a mortgage loan in August, your income for the year will show a substantial decrease over prior years. Your lender will probably not go to the trouble to figure out why. If this situation applies to you, figure out the percentage you earn late in the year and write a short letter detailing this.

> **Example:** You earn 75% of your income in the last half of the year. Your tax return for last year shows that you earned $40,000. You earned $10,000 from January through June, and $30,000 from July

through December. You apply for a loan at the end of June. Your yearly income shows that you have earned $15,000 through June. Your lender will use this as half your yearly income and project that you will earn $30,000 this year, a substantial decrease over last year. Actually, your projected income based on how you have earned your money in the past is $60,000, a substantial increase.

If you point this out in writing and attach it to your application, it should be considered. If you do not and your lender does not consider it, you will be rejected for insufficient income. Get a letter from your employer stating that what you are writing is true.

The opposite may also be true. If you sell gardening supplies, you may sell very little in the latter part of the year. A lender could look at your year-to-date income in July and conclude that you are going to make a lot more money this year than in the past. You should know the true picture so you do not get approved for a mortgage that you cannot afford.

Bonuses

The same applies to a bonus. If you get a yearly bonus in December and have been receiving it for several years without interruption, it should be counted as part of your income. If you apply in November, your year-to-date income will not look as good because of the lack of the bonus income. Write a short letter showing the amount of your bonuses over the past years (as many as possible). Get a letter from your employer stating that you have received these bonuses in the past years and that there is no reason to believe that this situation will end in the future.

Self-Employed

If you own your own business, you must document your income, as well as the income of your company. The lender will want to be confident that your business will not go under, leaving you without a job.

If you own your own business, it may be better to represent yourself as an employee of it as opposed to the owner.

Example: John bought a business several years ago. To celebrate, he decided to buy an expensive car. He wanted to finance part of the purchase price and proudly put down "owner" where the loan application asked for his title. The finance person at the dealership made him change it to "manager." He then got a letter from the company accountant saying that he worked for the company and stated his salary. Since no one checked the tax returns, no one questioned him and he got the loan. It would not have been this easy if he applied for a mortgage loan.

One of the oddities of mortgage approval occurs in the area of small business ownership. John, who bought the car, worked for the same company, whether he owned it or not. If you are a salaried employee of a company and show that you have been there for three years, you are considered a pretty good risk. There are seldom questions about how long the company has been in business and whether it is financially sound. No lender would consider asking a company to open its books before giving an employee a loan. If you show that you own a three-year-old business, you have to prove that it has a good chance to stay in business for the foreseeable future.

From the lender's perspective, there are additional risks in being an owner. The main one is debt. If you lose your job, you look for another. You may have to live off savings or even credit cards for a while, but that ends as soon as you find suitable employment. In most cases, owners of businesses will hang on long after they should have given up. They will beg and borrow from every possible source before finally closing. Once they finally do close the business, many are so far in debt that bankruptcy is the only answer. They may have borrowed on second or third mortgage loans. Since they know that they cannot pay on them all, they do not pay on any and foreclosure results.

Lenders understand these risks and do what they can to ensure themselves they are making a good loan. So, if the lender knows you are the owner of a business or if your business is such that you have no choice but to reveal that fact, be prepared to provide a lot more documentation.

If your business shows an increasing profit over the years and a seemingly bright future, gather both your individual and company tax returns for the last five years (or as long as you have owned the company if less than five years). As with the commission salesperson, document the seasonal aspect of your business if this is appropriate.

> **From the Expert**
>
> Your credit score and down payment will play a major role in the approval process. If the lender believes that you are personally reliable from your high credit score, it will help greatly.

If you are putting up a substantial down payment (20% or more), the lender may look more to the property for repayment than to you personally. Both a high credit score and large down payment will almost certainly get you approval, unless your business is very new or very shaky. You still may have to pay a little higher rate than if you were a salaried employee.

The second option is the easy one. Find a lender that does not require an examination of your business. These loans go by various names, such as *easy qualifier, stated income, low doc,* or *no doc.* There are differences between them, but the common element is that your income documentation is less. In the easiest ones, they simply take you at your word.

Again, your credit score and down payment will play the major roles. Lenders want to make loans. However, they do not just hand out money without regard as to whether it will be repaid. If you want them to ignore one aspect of the qualification process, such as income, you must be especially strong in the other areas of credit score and loan-to-value ratio.

Another option may be an FHA or VA loan. If you and the property qualify, you will find a more liberal underwriter. You will still need your documentation, but the guidelines for approval will not be as stringent.

Lenders now require you to give them permission to get your tax returns from the IRS. If they do not match the ones that you gave them, you will get rejected for the loan. You also may be criminally prosecuted for falsifying the returns. It is so easy with modern technology to make unnoticeable changes on documents that it is sometimes tempting to add a little income. Simply put, do not do it.

Gift Letters

Once you have documented all your income sources, it is also a good time to firm up any promises for help. As discussed earlier, a gift letter is a letter stating that you are receiving money for part of your down payment as a gift. The letter states the amount and that you have no obligation to repay. It is not a loan. Now is the time to contact that uncle who said that if you ever need money for a down payment on a home, he will be glad to help. If he was serious, draw up a gift letter and have him sign it.

Assets

The next step is to make a list of your *assets*. This should include cash, certificates of deposit, stocks, bonds, and anything else of value. If you are a collector, could you convert your collection to cash? Would you be willing to sell it off to help buy a home? If your assets are substantial, they may serve as a basis for setting loan approval.

If you have been putting your money into the stock market for several years and have an extensive portfolio, you may want to check with some stock brokers about a mortgage. Some brokerage houses are starting to offer mortgage loans up to 100% if you pledge your stock portfolio as security. This is a specialized area for those who truly believe that the market is the place to invest and have put most of their available cash into it. The value of your portfolio must be substantial. If you have over $100,000 in stocks, give it a try. More is usually required. (Charles Schwab Bank, for example, currently requires a minimum of $250,000.)

Remember that Wall Street is very competitive. Switching your account to a new brokerage may give you a better deal than dealing with your current brokerage. Call several of the large brokerage houses. The advantage to this type of borrowing is that you get to keep your stock. The disadvantage is that you may lose some control. They are not going to let you sell off your blue chips and buy high-risk shares.

The same possibility exists with CDs. You may be able to pledge them as part or all of your down payment. Check with your bank. The difference between stocks and CDs is that a good stock has a chance to increase

in value well beyond your interest rate on the mortgage. CDs will always be paying less than your mortgage interest rate on adjustable loans, unless rates rise beyond the cap on your ARM. That would normally require a huge jump in rates. The same applies for a fixed-rate loan.

The best way to use this option is if you have long-term CDs with a penalty for early withdrawal. You can use them to pay down your loan when they mature. Weigh the costs of the additional interest and possibly a higher interest rate against the cost of the penalty.

NOTE: *If a gift letter is a sure thing, count it as part of your assets.*

The important thing about your assets is to be realistic. Do not count on your stock going up when you need the cash or getting the highest possible price for your baseball card collection.

Spending

Getting your income documentation and asset list in order is the easy part. Now comes the real fun—documenting your spending.

Once you have figured out how much cash you could raise for a down payment, you should have an estimate of how much you can spend for a home. Use 20% as your starting point. If you have $30,000 to put down, divide that by 20%. This will give you $150,000 as an answer. If this seems reasonable for a home in your area, you have the whole spectrum of loans from which to choose. If this is unrealistic for your area, you know that you are going to need a loan with less than 20% down. If you divide $30,000 by 10%, you get $300,000. Is this realistic?

Play with the numbers. The greater the percentage you can put down, the more loans that are available to you. You should also include a cushion of a few percent for possible points and closing costs. You are also going to need moving money, and you do not want to move in without some money for unexpected expenses.

Examine Your Spending Habits

It is critical that you do the work described below. You are going to be dealing with real estate agents, and either lenders or mortgage brokers. They will all have the same goal — to get you a house and financing. The good ones will work very hard to get your offer accepted and get your mortgage loan approved at a fair price. But even the best of them will seldom warn you about possible problems in the future that will cause your loan to become so expensive that you could lose your home. If you do get such a warning, often it will come with the assurance that there is little chance that it could happen.

Another thing that they will seldom (if ever) do is go beyond the customary numbers. If your income-to-debt ratio is good enough to qualify you for the loan, that is where they will stop.

People lose their homes through foreclosure every day. Not all these losses are caused by job loss, illness, divorce, or death. Many are the result of irresponsible spending or taking on a mortgage that eventually required a higher payment than the borrower could afford.

> ### From the Expert
> You will not know what you can really afford to pay until you examine your spending habits.

Many people find the result of this examination very positive. They realize that by prioritizing their spending and cutting out or cutting down on some things that are really unimportant, they can afford much more than originally believed. This could mean the difference between getting a 15- or 20-year loan as opposed to a 30-year loan. The interest rate would be lower and the higher payments going to principal would save tens of thousands of dollars over the life of the loan.

At this point, you should have purchased a copy of your credit report from all three of the major credit bureaus — Equifax, Experian, and TransUnion. As discussed earlier in the book, you can contact these companies directly by telephone or on the Internet. (see p.15.) You can also use a service that will purchase all three for you. If you use a service, make sure it is not just a lender or mortgage broker trying to find a way to con-

tact potential customers. You do not want people pressuring you to take a loan from them quite yet.

Incidentally, many people get the wrong loan simply because they cannot say "no." If someone calls before you are ready, simply tell the person that you are not ready to discuss a loan yet. If they leave a phone number, you may call them at a future date. Ask them to please not call again. Whatever you do, do not start answering questions. If someone asks why you are not ready yet, you have to be strong enough to say that you are not going to explain your situation to him or her.

If you do not like confrontation, the easy way is simply to screen your calls on your answering machine. This will cause your phone to ring a lot more since the same people will keep calling, but at least you will not have to talk to them until you decide that the time is right.

You have to divide your spending into two categories—things that you must have (*necessities*) and so-called *discretionary spending*.

Unless you live in a city, such as New York, you probably own a car. How long could you keep that car if you were in a financial bind? Is it necessary that you have a relatively new car for business reasons or only for your own enjoyment? If you are making payments, when will they end? If you lease your car, can you roll over the lease and keep the car at a lower monthly payment? Contact your leasing company and find out if you can do this and how much the payment would be. This is not something that you will definitely do. It is only something that you could do if needed.

Have you financed anything else, like a big screen TV? Could you pay it off in a short time if needed? If you put the purchase on a credit card and make the minimum payment, as a practical matter, you will never pay it off.

Check your phone bill. Do you call mom across the country for an hour every day? Would she get too upset if you called her every other day?

Examine your credit card purchases. Are you paying interest on things that you could have purchased for cash, like a cup of coffee? Starbucks is trying out a program that allows a customer to swipe a credit card and leave. There is nothing to sign or identification to show, and it has a cur-

rent limit of $25. They would not do this unless there were a lot of customers buying coffee using a credit card.

What about the rest of your credit card purchases? Are there several items every month that are impulse buys that you later regret? Are you buying items from television infomercials or the channels that sell things all day? Get some idea of an average month's spending on the items that you really did not need.

Food can be a huge item. Some people eat dinner in a good restaurant three times a week. With a good (not great) bottle of wine, the cost for two is well over $15,000 a year. That is $1250 a month—not counting lunches or the Sunday breakfast. Add that amount onto a mortgage payment and see how drastically what you can afford changes.

Even things as seemingly minor as a morning cup of coffee and a pastry can add up. If you spend $6 every work day for coffee and a pastry, it comes to over $120 a month. If there are two of you doing this, the $240 a month could be the difference between a 30-year loan and a 20-year loan. Coffee and pastries are costing you several thousand dollars a year, in addition to the interest on your mortgage. It all comes down to what you want and your perspective.

Using Your New Knowledge

Once you start this process, you will think of many small items that fall into the category of unnecessary spending. Decide how many of these expenses could be cut back if needed and the total dollar amount saved. Now the important part—how will this benefit you?

First, you must realize that most of this will have no effect on your loan application. Paying off your car or credit cards will, of course, be considered by your lender. The rest of it will have no bearing on the underwriting process. It will, however, put you in a better position to choose the right loan.

If, with a better budget and a little self-restraint, you could save $400 per month without making your life unbearable, what are your choices? If you are getting a fixed-rate loan, can you afford a shorter term than

thirty years? You will get a lower interest rate, pay less interest because of the higher payment, and have a home free and clear in half the time.

If you do not want the required higher payment, you know that you can make additional principal payments on a 30-year loan of up to $400 per month. You will not save quite as much because your interest rate will be a little higher, but you will still cut both the amount of interest you pay and shorten the term.

> ### From the Expert
> A fixed-rate loan with a shorter term than thirty years is the single greatest money saver in a mortgage loan.

Additional principal payments that benefit you the most are also the most difficult to make. This is because they are most beneficial early in the loan term, when you are paying interest on the highest amount of principal. This is also when you are spending money to make your new home just the way you want it to be. You may be adding or replacing furniture and appliances, getting new carpeting and drapes, and so on. There is usually very little left over for additional principal payments. If you get the shorter term loan with the higher required payment, you may have to wait for that new dining room set, but you will save a lot of money.

Also, if you decide that an adjustable loan is best for you, you know that you can make a payment increase up to $400 per month if rates go up. If you choose a combination loan that is fixed for the first few years and then adjusts, you know that you can save $400 per month against the day when your payment may take a big jump. If your loan adjusts in five years, you will have a $24,000 cushion against the higher payment. That is not counting what you earn on the money. If rates go up, the amount could be $30,000 or more.

The final advantage is if you have some time before you need the loan. If you are planning to start looking for a home a year from now, you know how you can save an extra $4800 ($400 x 12). This could be the money that pays the point to buy down your interest rate. The lower rate could make the difference between qualifying and being rejected for the loan that you want.

As you know, unless you take the shorter term loan with the higher required payment, you will need to use some self-discipline. At least you will give yourself a chance that you probably would not have realized you had if you had not gone through this process.

The Other Side
The other aspect of the process can be disappointing, but still very useful. Suppose you discover that you are spending only on necessities or that tightening your belt would result in a savings of only $25 a month. You may not have all the same options or as much flexibility, but you still gain some valuable knowledge.

Now you know that getting an adjustable rate mortgage loan would most likely be an unacceptable risk. You may even want to rethink the price range of the home that you should buy. Any unexpected expense is going to cause a serious problem. You have no cushion. Knowing this could allow you to buy a home that you can keep.

Additional Comparisons
The final step is comparing your rent to the cost of a new home. If you are getting professional counseling, this will probably be covered. If not, be sure to ask what you should expect to be included in your total payment. Taxes, insurance, and other possible assessments are often required to be paid with your monthly principal and interest payment. Also, talk to as many people you know who own homes. Did they have any expenses beyond normal maintenance that hit them unexpectedly?

Even the location change should be considered. Are you moving farther from your work? Will there be any appreciable expense in commuting? The drive from Riverside, California to Los Angeles can cost you additional fuel and maintenance for your car. If you want to take advantage of the fast lane, you are going to have to pay the Fastrak toll. If you now have to take the train in from Connecticut to New York City, how much will it cost? Just as small savings can add up, small expenses add up too. Be sure to consider them.

Chapter 24

The Right Loan for You

Before getting into specific types of loans, you should be aware of the difference between A loans and B and C loans. The loans called *A loans* are for borrowers without serious qualification problems. There are differences among A loans, but they are usually small. The relative strength of the borrower may result in an interest rate difference of .125% to .5%. This difference could also be from using the wrong lender or an incompetent mortgage broker.

If you do not qualify for an A loan, you drop to the B or C category. The B and C categories are for borrowers whose credit scores or history does not allow them to be in the preferred A category. In these categories, the rate difference becomes more significant, usually 2%–3%.

You will know when a potential lender tells you the rate that they want to charge you whether it is in the A category. If you are not sure, ask. If it is not, ask for specific reasons why. Then talk to a mortgage broker. Mortgage brokers have access to many lenders, where a direct lender only serves one bank. A competent, experienced broker should know if you can get an A loan from any lender. If not, he or she may be able to suggest some things you could do to qualify, like paying off a few small bills. Do not settle for less than an A loan before you have exhausted the possibilities of getting one.

Now that you understand the factors that go into gathering a loan and what mortgages are all about, you need to decide which type is best for you.

Fixed Interest Rate Loans

If you believe that interest rates will soon be on the rise, a fixed-rate loan will give you the security of a set interest rate and payment. Since most lenders believe that rates will rise, you will have to pay more for the fixed rate. Some lenders or mortgage brokers may try to talk you into some type of an adjustable loan, which they believe will be advantageous for them.

The fixed-rate loan is the one you should use as your basis of comparison with any and all types of adjustable rate loans. Because of this, it is critical to know the best fixed-rate loan that you can get. If you do not, your comparison with adjustable rate loans will be skewed.

You should always ask your lender or mortgage broker if you are getting the best rate being offered. Make it clear that you are not asking if this is the best rate *you* can get. You want to know if it is the best rate *anyone* can get. If the answer is no, ask for the specific reasons why you are less credit worthy than the strongest borrower. If you believe any of the drawbacks to getting the best rate can be rectified, ask what you must do to qualify for the best rate.

Always get specific information. If the lender tells you that your debt ratio is too high, go through your debts with the lender to see which ones you need to pay down or pay off. The extra money you saved from examining your spending habits may be used to get a better loan.

The Break-Even Buydown

Once you are convinced that you are getting the best rate you can get, ask about a *buydown*. You need to know how much it will cost, how much less the interest rate will be, and how long the lower rate will last. Then you do a simple calculation comparing the options.

Example: On a $200,000 loan at 6.5%, your first payment would have $1,083.33 going to interest. At a rate of 6.25%, $1,041.67 goes to interest. The difference is roughly $40. If you were to pay one point to lower the rate, it would cost you $2000. At $40 per month, it would take fifty months to break even—little over four years.

The break-even date has one more consideration. How much could you earn on the $2000 if you did not pay it as a point to buy down your loan? If you invested it in a successful stock, you would make much more than you would save on the buydown. However, you could also lose some of it.

> **Example:** If you took the $2000 and put it in a CD at 3% interest, compounded monthly for four years, it would pay $254.66 in interest. If this is the rate available to you, your break-even date now has to be extended for roughly an additional 6½ months, figuring your savings at $40 per month.

Do not be afraid to use rough figures and numbers in your head or with pencil and paper. Since each of these situations involve some level of uncertainty, you want to be able to throw out the obviously bad options without wasting a lot of time. If you are not sure of your numbers, ask the lender or broker to figure out the break-even time for you once you are down to those that you will seriously consider.

Once you know the break-even date, you simply have to determine what the chances are that you will keep the loan that long. If rates are falling, you do not want to buy down. You are probably going to refinance before the break-even date. If you believe rates are going to rise, it would be beneficial to keep the loan. Now your consideration turns to another decision. Will you sell the home before the break-even date?

Things to consider are a possible job transfer, increasing family size, school changes, and so on. There are many reasons why you may move. You can only make an educated guess as to whether you will before the break-even date.

Adjustable Rate Mortgages

Now that you are armed with your qualification information and your fixed-rate loan information, you can begin making comparisons with the different types of adjustable rate loans. Before getting into specifics, you should be aware of the value of the annual percentage rate (APR). You may

have noticed that you have not been asked to consider it. The APR is the interest rate plus certain costs, such as points, expressed as a percentage.

Example: Look at a 6% loan with one point and no fees for one year. Since a point is 1%, you can see that the APR would be 7%, which is the interest rate plus the point. (It is slightly less, but close.) The same interest rate and point with a change in the term from one year to five years changes the APR to 6.415%. At thirty years, the APR is 6.093%.

You can see the problem. About 5% of all 30-year loans last for thirty years. The percentage is probably smaller now after the wave of refinancing over the last few years. Basing your borrowing decisions on the APR is assuming that you will keep your loan for its entire term. It hardly ever happens with 30-year loans. If you are getting a short-term loan that you intend to keep for its full term, the APR is a very valuable tool.

The requirement that the APR be disclosed was especially helpful for loans for cars and appliances. It alerted shoppers to the use of *add-on* loans, in which interest was figured so that a 6% interest rate could actually cost the borrower 12%. These practices are not used in home mortgages. The APR for long-term mortgage loans is much less useful than figuring out break-even dates.

Beginning Your Comparison

Once you have established how much you will pay on the best fixed-rate loan you can get, start getting quotes on adjustable rate loans. The first rule is to ignore the start rate unless it is the only way you can qualify. If this is the case, you cannot compare the adjustable to the fixed-rate loan because you cannot qualify for the fixed-rate loan at the amount that you are trying to borrow. If you are still determined to borrow this amount, ask the following questions.

- How much will the rate be after the start rate ends?
- What will be the amount of your monthly payment once that happens?

Do not settle for the answer that it depends on the rate at the time of adjustment. You want to know the rate and payment based on rates today. You then want to know the adjustment period and how it will affect your payment if it adjusts to the maximum allowed during each period. Follow the adjustment up to the cap. In other words, if the loan over the years adjusts to the maximum rate, what will be the interest rate and the monthly payment? Will this payment amortize over the term or will there be a balloon payment due?

In order to weigh the risk of the interest rate going all the way up to the cap, you have to know which index will be used. If the lender is using a lagging indicator, such as COFI, there is less chance that it will rise to the cap. Even if it does, it will take much longer to get there than a leading indicator. This at least gives you more time to increase your income or eliminate other debts.

Review Your Spending Analysis

Once you have all this information, go back to your spending analysis. Could you afford to make the highest possible payment by cutting out unnecessary spending? If the answer is no, you are going to depend on interest rates not going up to the maximum, your income increasing or paying off current debts to free up some cash. You may decide to take the risk. Many, if not most borrowers, do not even know the risk.

If there is no problem with qualifying, you still make the same analysis. You are, of course, in a better situation. You are now trying to determine which loan will cost you the least without considering whether you can get the loan. Ignoring the start rate, you compare break-even dates for each type of adjustable loan.

For loans that are fixed for three, five, seven, or even ten years and then adjust, you have to compare the cost of each. You compare the rates, fees, and any prepayment penalties for these loans based on how long you intend to keep the loan. You should base paying off the loan on selling the property rather than refinancing. Rates for 2005 and beyond are expected to go up. Do not count on getting a better loan within the next several years. Again, be sure to consider the index.

Make the Comparison

Once you have found the best adjustable rate loan for your time period, compare it to the fixed-rate loan. The time period is the critical part. Using the worst case scenario, the adjustable rate loan will never be better than the fixed-rate loan over the full term. The general rule is that the adjustable will almost always be better if paid off within five years, depending on a possible prepayment penalty. Extending it a few years more gets into uncertainty.

There are two variables that have to be considered. Whether rates will rise, fall, or stay stable is the first major consideration. If you believe that the economy is entering a period of rapidly increasing interest rates, the fixed-rate loan is the obvious choice. If you believe interest rates may rise, but not too much or too fast, an adjustable loan—especially one using a lagging indicator—may be acceptable. Falling rates favor the adjustable loan since it is cheaper for the first few years and you will probably refinance as rates go down.

The second variable is how long you intend to keep the loan. Generally, shorter periods favor the adjustable loan. You can see that there are decisions to make based upon future occurrences. Since the future cannot be predicted with absolute accuracy, you cannot be absolutely sure that the loan you get will turn out to be the least expensive over the years. Preparing yourself to make the decision based on solid information, rather than advertising and lures of low payments, will most likely make your decision the correct one.

Lenders and Mortgage Brokers

Finally, in selecting the right loan, you need to choose the right lender or mortgage broker. Finding the right person to deal with is probably the most important thing you can do to get the best loan. A competent and honest person will find you the best possible loan and charge you a fair price for the service.

If you have your down payment money, you will be given any number of the different programs being offered. You will be treated well because of your available down payment and should get answers to all your questions.

If you have access to a credit union, see what they are offering. Credit unions usually do not offer many mortgage loan programs, so it is fairly easy to compare what they offer to your bank or savings and loan's programs.

The last, and sometimes the best choice, is a mortgage broker. An independent mortgage broker has access to thousands of loan programs. If you get a competent and experienced one, he or she will eliminate the ones that are difficult to work with and will know where you can get the best loan for your situation.

Many large lenders have subsidiary mortgage companies. The employees may be simply funneling loans to specific programs. You want to deal with someone who has the freedom to place your loan with the lender that has the best deal.

If you use a broker to help you sort through all the available options, you will be involved with *back points*. These are fees paid to brokers by lenders, based on the interest rate.

Example: A lender may offer the broker one point on a 6% loan and two points on a 6.25% loan. The broker then tells the borrower that the best loan available is at 6.25% and makes the higher commission. An up-front, ethical broker will tell the borrower in advance how much will be charged. If 1%, the borrower gets the 6% loan. If 2%, the broker will tell the borrower that to get a 2% commission, the borrower has to pay 6.25%. The borrower can then choose to pay one point out-of-pocket to the broker and get the 6% loan or may want to pay the two points out-of-pocket and get an even lower rate.

The advantage is that knowing how much the broker is charging lets the borrower make decisions. You may believe that the commission is too high and seek a different broker. If you are not told the commission

amount like in the above example, you may believe that you are paying one point when you are actually paying two. In so-called *no points loans,* you could, in effect, be paying two points when you believe that you are not paying any.

The borrower may ask the broker to lower the commission. There is a lot of work involved in putting together a loan package. If you have outstanding credit and income-to-debt ratios, and are putting down 20% or more, you may ask the broker to slightly lower the commission. If you have any problems that require special handling by the broker, he or she has probably more than earned the usual commission. Whatever the situation, know the broker's fee and get a written commitment that the fee will not change.

Mortgage Comparison Worksheet

Use this worksheet used to compare your possible loans. Start with the fixed-rate loan as Loan 1. Loan 2 would then be the fixed-rate loan with a buydown. Loans 3, 4, and 5 would be the adjustable or hybrid loans that you have selected as the best ones to consider. The monthly payment and the break-even period are included at the bottom of the chart to emphasize the true monthly payment and not the start rate payment. A teaser interest rate has not been added, as the less emphasis you put on it the better.

Mortgage Comparison Worksheet

	Loan 1	Loan 2	Loan 3	Loan 4	Loan 5
Type of Loan					
Loan Amount					
Term					
Fixed Term					
Adjustment Period					
Interest Adjustment Cap per Period					
Total Cap					
Payment Adjustment Period					
Cap per Period					
Total Payment Cap					
Index					
Margin					
Total Real Interest Rate					
Points					
Total Points and Fees					
Start Rate Payment					
True Monthly Payment					
Break-Even Period					

Conclusion

It is not an easy task to get the absolutely best mortgage loan for you. By due diligence, however, you can get a good loan. The following are important requirements to get the best loan you can.

- Look at the loan in its entirety, not just the low start rate or low beginning monthly payment. This will help you avoid being drawn in by ads for teaser rates and low monthly payments that cost you more in the long run.
- Have all the prequalifying information in writing before you start shopping for a home or a mortgage loan. This includes your credit report and any explanations you may have for credit problems. Do not count on a loan representative or mortgage broker to tell your story to the underwriter. If you write it down and it goes in the package, you have a good chance that underwriting may consider it.
- Make a genuine effort to realistically know what you could pay on an adjustable loan if rates increased. This can only be done by a careful examination of your debts and spending habits.
- Consult with an independent counselor whenever possible. Be sure that the counselor is truly independent—not someone recommended by your lender or mortgage broker.
- Above all, do not sign anything that you do not understand, and get all promises in writing whenever possible. It is easy to make verbal promises. Most people do not write them down unless they intend to keep them. Always write down the name of the person that you talk to on the phone.

Finally, good luck in finding the right mortgage loan for you.

Glossary

1031 Exchange. A procedure used to avoid paying tax on the profit from the sale of investment property by *trading* currently-owned property for other property. It is not really an exchange, since it does not have to be concurrent and the owners do not have to end up with each other's property. Specific IRS rules must be followed or the profit becomes taxable income.

A

additional principal payments. Payments that are higher than the required amount. The extra money reduces the principal balance.

adjustable rate mortgage (ARM). A mortgage with an interest rate that changes as the rate of an index changes.

adjustment period. The time between possible changes to the rate of interest for an adjustable rate mortgage.

all-inclusive deed of trust. *See wraparound mortgage.*

amortization. Paying both principal and interest at the required payment amount to pay off the loan according to an agreed-upon schedule.

annual percentage rate. The interest rate plus certain costs of borrowing expressed as a percentage.

appraisal. An estimate of value of real property at a certain date made by a person acceptable to the parties involved as qualified to make the estimate.

assumable mortgage. A mortgage that allows a buyer to replace the seller by taking over the obligation of the loan.

B

back points. A commission paid to a mortgage broker that is not charged as points to the borrower. The borrower will pay a higher rate of interest to make up for the commission payment.

balloon payment mortgage. A mortgage that has required payments not sufficient to pay it off (amortize it) during the term. As a consequence, the final payment is much larger than prior payments. This large payment is the balloon.

beneficiary. The word used for the lender when a deed of trust is the loan document.

biweekly payment mortgage. A mortgage loan requiring half the agreed upon monthly payment every two weeks. This results in a larger amount being paid each month, which reduces the principal balance and the length of the term.

blanket mortgage. A mortgage that secures more than one piece of property. It is commonly used by builders for construction of a tract of land.

bridge loan. A temporary loan to buy time for the borrower until money from another source (a more permanent loan or sale of property) is obtained.

buydown. A payment of a lump sum of money to a lender to reduce the interest rate of a loan. The reduced rate may be for the life of the loan, or more commonly, for the first few years of the loan.

buyer's market. A situation that occurs when demand for homes is low and sellers are willing to accept offers that are favorable to the buyer.

C
certificate of eligibility. A document issued by the Veterans Administration showing that a specific veteran may apply for a VA guaranteed mortgage.

certificate of reasonable value. The name for the appraisal used for a VA guaranteed mortgage.

closing costs. The costs of a loan separate from interest. These include the cost of escrow, title insurance, and so on.

collateral security. The mortgaged property. When a person borrows money, the loan is secured by the promise to repay. When the lender requires more security, such as real estate, the property is the collateral security.

commission points. Percentage charged to compensate the lender or mortgage broker for services.

commitment. 1. A guarantee by a lender that the borrower will get a loan on the specified terms. 2. A preliminary report by a title company guaranteeing title insurance if certain specified conditions are met.

condominium. A form of subdivision setting forth the area owned by each individual unit owner and having all owners of units own the remaining area in common. Although there is no specific architectural requirement, most projects have common walls and roofs. The common area may be extensive and include swimming pools, tennis courts, a clubhouse, and so on, or may consist of the units with virtually no common area.

conforming loan. A loan that follows the Fannie Mae or Freddie Mac guidelines for sale in the secondary market.

conventional mortgage. A mortgage not made, insured, or guaranteed by a government agency.

convertible ARMs. Adjustable rate mortgages that can convert to fixed-rate loans at a future date.

consolidation loan. A mortgage loan used to pay off other debts, such as car loans and credit cards. The purpose is to lower the interest rate and monthly payments of the borrower from the higher interest rate loans to the mortgage interest rate.

contingency clause. Wording in a contract that makes it unenforceable if specified conditions are not met. Common examples are clauses that state that a buyer is not obligated to buy property until and unless he or she is able to sell currently owned property, or that the buyer is not obligated to buy property if he or she is unable to get a mortgage loan for a certain amount.

cooperative. A type of subdivision in which the property owners own stock in the real estate project, with each given the exclusive right to occupy a unit. Also called a *stock cooperative*.

credit bureau. A company that compiles records of a person's debts, and whether these debts were repaid as agreed.

credit history. The record of borrowing by a person and whether these debts were repaid as agreed.

credit repository. *See credit bureau.*

credit score. A number derived by a formula that rates a person's credit history.

cross-collateral. Hypothecating additional property to obtain a mortgage. For example, the borrower does not have sufficient equity in the home to get the desired loan, so he or she puts up a vacation home as additional security.

D

deed in lieu of foreclosure. A deed given by the property owner to a lender instead of the lender going through the foreclosure process. Its purpose is to save the time and expense of foreclosure when the borrower has little or no equity in the property.

deed of trust. A document used in some states instead of a mortgage. It has the same purpose as a mortgage, but is structured differently.

deficiency judgment. A personal debt owed to a lender by a borrower after the foreclosure sale of the mortgaged property did not bring the total amount owed. Nonrecourse mortgages do not allow deficiency judgments.

delinquency. An amount that was paid later than agreed or not paid at all.

discount points. The percentage paid to reduce the interest rate to a borrower or a reduction from face value in order to sell a loan in the secondary mortgage market.

down payment. The cash portion of a property purchase. The amount between the purchase price and the mortgage loan amount.

due on sale clause. Wording in a mortgage that gives the lender the right to demand full payment of the loan if the mortgaged property is sold.

E

equity skimming. A scam usually perpetrated by buying property from an owner during the foreclosure process for a small amount of money, then renting the property until foreclosure is completed and the tenants are evicted by the new owner. The skimmer, also called a *milker*, does not turn over the rent to the lender, but keeps it for personal use. A less common type of skimming is when the mortgagor moves out, rents the property during foreclosure, and does not pay the rent to the lender but keeps it for personal use.

escrow account. Money paid by the mortgagor to the mortgagee in addition to principal and interest, so that the lender can pay taxes (and sometimes insurance) when due.

F

Fannie Mae. The Federal National Mortgage Association. A major purchaser of loans in the secondary mortgage market.

federal reserve. The Board of Governors of the Federal Reserve System, among other duties, set interest rates for borrowing by banks. These rates have an effect on mortgage rates.

fees. Money charged by lenders and others involved in mortgage loan transactions, as distinguished from interest on the loan.

FICO. The Fair Isaacs Corporation credit score.

fixed payment loan. A loan that requires a level payment. Other terms of the loan may change.

fixed-rate loan. A loan that will require the borrower to pay the same interest rate for the entire term.

fixer-upper. A property requiring repair or remodeling to bring it to what is considered standard condition. The term is used in advertising to imply that the property is priced lower than similar properties in good condition.

flexible payment mortgage. A loan that requires the payment to adjust at some time during the term to amortize the loan. The adjustment can cause a huge increase in the payment since there is no cap on the payment.

forbearance. The lender's delaying foreclosure to allow the borrower to make up delinquencies, refinance, or sell the property. It may include the forgiveness of past-due interest.

foreclosure. The process brought by a lender of selling property at auction to pay a mortgage loan in default. The procedure varies depending on the type of mortgage and the state where the property is located.

Freddie Mac. The Federal Home Loan Mortgage Corporation. A stockholder owned corporation, originally chartered by Congress, that buys mortgage loans in the secondary mortgage market.

fully-indexed rate. The total interest charged to the borrower for an adjustable rate loan once the start rate ends. It includes the interest rate of the index and the margin.

G

gap loan. A temporary loan to supply needed money before a sale or longer term financing can be completed. It is arranged quickly, easy to get, and expensive.

gift letter. A letter from one who is giving money to a buyer for part of the down payment. The letter must state that the money need not be repaid.

Ginnie Mae. The Government National Mortgage Association. A government agency that guarantees payment to those who buy certain types of mortgage backed securities.

graduated payment mortgage. A mortgage loan that begins with a low monthly payment that gradually increases to an amount necessary to amortize the loan over the term. Its purpose is to help buyers who expect future income to increase.

H

hard money mortgage. 1. A mortgage loan with interest and fees much higher than market rates and fees. It allows borrowing by those who cannot get a loan elsewhere because of severe credit or debt problems. 2. A mortgage loan that is not used to purchase property.

holder in due course. One who buys a negotiable instrument, such as a mortgage note. The buyer gets certain legal protections greater than the originator of the loan. To become a holder in due course, procedures described in the Uniform Commercial Code must be followed.

home equity conversion mortgage (HECM). The name for the FHA insured version of a reverse mortgage.

home equity line of credit. A mortgage loan that allows the borrower to draw money to a maximum amount at any time during the term. Interest

is paid only on the amount borrowed. The money may be repaid and borrowed again at any time during the term. It is a revolving loan, similar to a credit card loan.

home equity loan. A loan not used to purchase property. It is usually secured by a second mortgage and covers the equity between the first mortgage and the property value.

home keeper mortgage. The name given to the Fannie Mae version of a reverse mortgage.

HUD. The Department of Housing and Urban Development. FHA is one of its many departments.

hybrid mortgage loan. A mortgage loan that contains both fixed and adjustable periods during the term.

hypothecate. To put up property as collateral security without the physical delivery of the property, as is done with a mortgage loan. When the property is physically held by the lender as security, it is pledged.

I

income-to-debt ratios. The comparison of a prospective borrower's income to debt expressed as a percentage. The *top* ratio is the comparison of the income to PITI monthly mortgage costs. The *bottom* ratio is the comparison of income to total monthly debt payments.

indexes. The products that are used to set interest rates for adjustable mortgage loans. These include such things as Treasury Bill rates and others that are publicly published. Some, like T-Bill rates and the prime rate, are volatile and are called *leading* indexes. Others, like COFI, change more slowly and are called *lagging* indexes.

impound account. *See escrow account.*

interest. The amount paid for the use of money. The rate is expressed as a percentage.

interest only mortgage loan. A loan requiring the borrower to make monthly payments covering only the interest on the loan and requiring a lump-sum principal payment called a balloon. Principal reduction is on a voluntary basis until the term ends.

J

jumbo loan. A mortgage loan above the limits of Fannie Mae and Freddie Mac. It is a *nonconforming* loan.

junior mortgage. A mortgage in a secondary or lesser position than a first mortgage.

L

loan commitment. *See commitment.*

loan-to-value ratio. The ratio, expressed as a percentage, of the loan amount to the value of the mortgaged property.

locked-in rate. The interest rate on a mortgage loan that the lender has agreed to use if the loan closes within a specified time.

M

margin. The portion of the interest rate over the index rate. It is the profit to the lender.

milking. *See equity skimming.*

modified tenure. A reverse mortgage program allowing the borrower to take a portion of the loan amount as a lump sum and the balance in lifetime payments.

modified term. A reverse mortgage program that allows the borrower to take a portion of the loan amount as a lump sum and the balance in payments over a specified term.

modification. A change made to an existing contract. When the term is used as a method to avoid foreclosure, it means that the lender agrees to change the terms of the loan so that the borrower can make the payments. The change could be lowering the interest rate, forgiving delinquent interest, or any other change to help the borrower cure the default.

mortgage calculator. Any of a number of programs designed to supply information on various aspects of mortgage lending, such as amortization schedules, monthly payments at various interest rates, or savings on prepayment.

mortgage loan application. The supplying of financial information by a borrower to a lender to help the lender decide whether to make a mortgage loan and which loan program it can offer.

mortgage-backed securities. Bonds issued by secondary lenders that are secured by mortgages. The sale of these instruments replenishes the supply of money to the secondary mortgage market.

mortgage banker. A mortgage company that makes portfolio mortgage loans or loans to be sold in the secondary market, as opposed to simply brokering the loans.

mortgage broker. A person or company that facilitates obtaining a mortgage loan. The broker puts together the loan package for submission to a lender and charges a fee for the service. The cost to the borrower may be

less than dealing directly with a lender, since the broker can shop the package and has access to hundreds of lenders.

mortgagee. The lender that receives a mortgage in exchange for making a loan.

mortgage insurance premium (MIP). The required insurance payment for an FHA loan. The insurance is to protect the lender from a loss if the borrower defaults.

mortgagor. The borrower that gives a mortgage to a lender to secure repayment of a loan.

mortgage pass-through securities. *See mortgage-backed securities.*

N

negotiable instrument. A debt instrument that may be transferred (sold) using procedures set out by the Uniform Commercial Code. The buyer incurs less liability than the originator of the instrument. Mortgage notes are negotiable instruments.

nonconforming loan. A loan that does not fall within the guidelines of Fannie Mae or Freddie Mac for sale to the secondary market.

nonrecourse mortgage. A mortgage loan under which the borrower is not personally liable if the mortgaged property does not bring enough money at the foreclosure to cover what is owed.

note. A debt instrument by which the borrower promises to repay money. A mortgage is used to secure the promise.

notice of default. An instrument giving notice that a mortgage loan borrower is in default. The document is recorded and becomes a matter of public record. The notice is required to begin foreclosure proceedings.

O

original lender. The retail lender that makes the mortgage loan to the borrower. The loan can either be kept as a portfolio loan or sold to a secondary lender.

origination fee. A fee, usually expressed in points, paid to the retail lender for services.

P

piggyback loan. A second mortgage loan offered with the first loan. The purpose is to reduce the first loan to 80% so PMI is not required.

principal, interest, taxes, and insurance (PITI). The costs used to determine the top loan income-to-debt ratio.

planned unit development (PUD). A subdivision with lots the same size or nearly the same size as the buildings on them. The owner of each unit owns the lot under the unit, and owns the remainder of the subdivision in common with the other unit owners.

points. Another way of expressing certain costs of a mortgage loan. Each point is equal to one percent of the loan amount.

portfolio loan. A loan that will be kept by the originating lender and not sold in the secondary market.

preapproval. Agreement by a lender to make a mortgage loan for a certain maximum amount without considering the specific property the borrower may purchase. It does not lock in the interest rate and is not a firm commitment to make the loan.

prepayment penalty. An extra cost to the borrower if the loan is repaid sooner than required. The repayment time and penalty amount are not standard and not applicable to all loans.

prequalifying. An estimate by a lender of the amount and type of loan for which a borrower may be eligible. It is given before the application and documentation is submitted, and is not binding on the lender. The term may also be used for the research done by a prospective borrower to estimate the amount and type of mortgage loan he or she may be qualified to expect.

primary lender. The lender who originates the loan, also called the originating lender or retail lender. The term is used to distinguish this lender from one that buys the loan in the secondary market.

primary residence. An inexact term that describes the home in which the borrower *lives*, as opposed to a vacation property. The common requirement is that the borrower spends most of the year at that location. Intent may also be considered. Mortgage loans are less expensive and easier to qualify for if the property to be mortgaged is the primary residence of the borrower.

principal. 1. The amount owed on a mortgage loan without considering interest. 2. A person who uses an agent. An owner of property is the principal. The real estate broker or mortgage broker is the agent of that person.

private mortgage insurance (PMI). A protection for the lender that it will not suffer a loss if the amount owed on the mortgage loan exceeds what the lender receives at a foreclosure sale. The policy does not cover the entire loan amount. The insurance is required when a borrower's down payment is less than 20%.

promissory note. A debt instrument under which the debtor promises to pay a certain amount of money at a specific date or on demand. A mortgage is given to secure payment.

purchase money mortgage. 1. A mortgage given to a seller by a buyer as part of the down payment or to secure any part or the entire selling price of the property. 2. Any mortgage, the proceeds of which are used to

purchase the mortgaged property, as distinguished from an equity loan or refinance loan.

R

recasting. A method of refiguring both the interest rate and monthly payment at a specific time in the loan term. The payment becomes the amount necessary to amortize the loan in the time remaining on the term. Depending on the original interest rate and payment agreement, recasting can increase the monthly payment by 100% or more. There is no cap when a loan is recast.

recourse. The ability of a lender to look to the borrower to be personally responsible for the loss suffered if the sale of the mortgaged property from foreclosure does not cover the amount owed.

refinancing. Paying off an existing mortgage loan and replacing it with a new loan. The term is also used to describe getting a mortgage loan other than to purchase the property, even if there is no existing mortgage to be paid off.

Regulation Z. A part of the *Truth in Lending Act* requiring disclosure of the cost of a loan to a borrower.

relinquished property. In a tax-deferred property exchange, the property sold by the taxpayer.

replacement property. In a tax-deferred exchange, the property purchased by the taxpayer.

Real Estate Settlement Procedures Act (RESPA). A federal law prohibiting certain unfair lending practices, such as kickbacks and requiring disclosure of costs for services performed.

reverse mortgage. A mortgage loan whereby the borrower receives money but is not obligated to repay it until no longer residing at the mortgaged property. Under current law, a borrower must be age 62 to qualify. All reverse mortgage loans are nonrecourse loans.

S

shared appreciation mortgage (SAM). A loan that entitles the lender to part of the profit from the future sale of the property. The property may also be refinanced at the future date to pay off the lender, with the profit based on the appraised value.

secondary lender. One that purchases an existing mortgage loan rather than the lender that originates the loan.

secondary mortgage market. The buying and selling of existing mortgage loans.

second mortgage. The loan behind a first mortgage. The sequence in which the loans were made and recorded determines which is first or second. The amount of the loan is not considered.

seller's market. A period during which there is a high demand for homes, creating an advantage to sellers. Prices rise in a seller's market.

servicing agent. The one from whom the borrower receives the monthly statement and makes the payment, if different from the mortgagee.

settlement costs. *See closing costs.*

short sale. Acceptance by a lender of an amount less than the total owed on a mortgage loan as full payment. The purpose is to avoid the time and cost of foreclosure. The most common use of a short sale is when there is little or no equity in the property and little or no chance of collecting on a deficiency judgment.

singlefile mortgage. A program for borrowers under which the lender pays the PMI and passes the cost to the borrower in the interest rate.

start rate. The interest rate at the beginning of an adjustable rate mortgage loan. The rate lasts for a short period and then changes to the permanent rate formula of the index plus margin.

stock cooperative. *See cooperative.*

subject-to-mortgage takeover. The purchase of mortgaged property by one who acknowledges that there is a mortgage but assumes no liability for it. It differs from an assumption, under which the buyer agrees to pay the loan.

T

teaser rate. *See start rate.*

tenure. In a reverse mortgage, it is the term used to describe the program by which the borrower receives income for as long as he or she occupies the property as a primary residence.

term. The length of a mortgage loan.

trust deed. *See deed of trust.*

trustee. In a deed of trust, one who holds title to the property for purposes of issuing a reconveyance or instituting foreclosure proceedings.

trustor. The borrower under a deed of trust.

two-step mortgage. A program that calls for a one-time adjustment in the interest rate of the mortgage loan after five or seven years. Once the loan adjusts, there are no further changes for the rest of the term.

U

underwriting. The process used by a lender to evaluate the application of a borrower seeking to get a mortgage loan.

V

variable rate mortgage. *See adjustable rate mortgage.*

W

workout assumption. The taking over of a mortgage loan in default, even though the loan may say it cannot be assumed. The purpose is to avoid foreclosure, and the workout may include some forgiveness of unpaid interest.

wraparound mortgage. A junior mortgage that has a face amount of the amount borrowed plus the amount owed on the existing mortgage. For example, the borrower owes $50,000 on an existing mortgage. He or she now borrows an additional $10,000, but gives a mortgage for $60,000. The borrower makes payments on the second mortgage based on $60,000, and the lender makes the payment on the underlying mortgage of $50,000. Different interest rates of the wraparound and underlying mortgage may make it more advantageous than refinancing.

Appendix A

Amoritization Tables

The following amortization schedules compare the first five years of a $250,000 loan with interest rates of 6%, 6.5%, and 7%, both for thirty years and fifteen years. There is also a table that shows the first five years of a 7%, 30-year loan with an additional $100 per month prepaid. There are three aspects that you should compare.

The first is the *monthly payment*. The difference between the 6% loan and the 7% loan is approximately $165 (rounded off). Over five years that equates to $9,900. At the end of five years, in spite of the higher payment, you would owe $2693 more on the 7% loan than on the 6% loan. Rounding off to $2700, the 7% loan would cost you $12,600 more than the 6% loan over the first five years. If you were to buy down the interest rate from 7% to 6% for the first five years of the loan, you would have $12,600 to work with. For example, if you could buy down the loan from 7% to 6% for two points ($5000), you would most likely come out ahead. This is because putting the $5000 into another investment would probably not earn you $7,600 in five years — the amount you would need to break even.

The second comparison is the possibility of a *lower interest rate* by reducing the term. If the best you can get on a 30-year loan is 7%, you can probably get 6.5% on a 15-year loan.

The drawback is that your payment will be approximately $514 more. Over a five-year period, that totals $30,840. If you can afford it, there is an upside: After five years paying on the 30-year, 7% loan, you will owe $232,635. On the 15-year, 6.5% loan, you will owe $192,792. The difference

between the payment amount ($30,840) and the savings on interest ($39,843) is almost exactly $9000. If you invested the $514 monthly for five years, you would have to get over a 9% return to end up with $9000.

The third consideration is *equity building*. If, after five years, you want to sell or refinance your home, you are certainly in a better position if you owe $192,792 than if you owe $232,635. Building equity protects you against market changes and personal economic changes. You may never need to use your equity for an emergency, but it is nice to know it is there just in case.

The last table shows a 7%, 30-year loan with an additional principal payment of $100 per month. Over sixty months (five years), $100 per month totals $6000. The amount owed after five years is $228,169—$7159 less than the same loan without the additional payments. You saved $1159 in interest. In order to get $1159 by investing the $6000 elsewhere, you would need a return of over 19%. Any additional principal payments during the first few years of a mortgage loan are almost always a good investment.

If you look at the table from the standpoint of equity building, the result is also impressive. Your balance on the 7% loan with the $100 per month additional principal payment is $4,466 less than the 30-year, 6% loan with no additional payments.

To follow through for the full thirty years, the following is the breakdown.

Total interest paid over the life of the loan (no prepayment): $348,772
Total interest paid over the life of the loan (with prepayment): $281,993
Total interest saved: $66,778
            Shortening of the loan term: 4 years, 10 months

Remember, you have paid an additional $25,200 (25 years, 10 months) in payments over the life of the loan, reducing your savings to $41,578— still substantial.

To fully appreciate the savings, you would also have to deduct what you could have made by investing the money elsewhere and take into consideration deductions for tax purposes. In spite of this, the numbers are impressive enough that unless you have a place to put your money that most people do not have, you are better off making additional principal payments.

First Five Years of a 6%, 30-year loan

Principal	Payment	APR	Total Interest	Total Loan Value
$250,000.00	$1,498.88	6.0000%	$289,596.80	$539,596.80

Payment	Principal	Interest	Balance
1	$248.88	$1,250.00	$249,751.12
2	$250.12	$1,248.76	$249,501.00
3	$251.38	$1,247.50	$249,249.62
4	$252.63	$1,246.25	$248,996.99
5	$253.90	$1,244.98	$248,743.09
6	$255.16	$1,243.72	$248,487.93
7	$256.44	$1,242.44	$248,231.49
8	$257.72	$1,241.16	$247,973.77
9	$259.01	$1,239.87	$247,714.76
10	$260.31	$1,238.57	$247,454.45
11	$261.61	$1,237.27	$247,192.84
12	$262.92	$1,235.96	$246,929.93
13	$264.23	$1,234.65	$246,665.69
14	$265.55	$1,233.33	$246,400.14
15	$266.88	$1,232.00	$246,133.26
16	$268.21	$1,230.67	$245,865.05
17	$269.55	$1,229.33	$245,595.50
18	$270.90	$1,227.98	$245,324.59
19	$272.26	$1,226.62	$245,052.34
20	$273.62	$1,225.26	$244,778.72
21	$274.99	$1,223.89	$244,503.73
22	$276.36	$1,222.52	$244,227.37
23	$277.74	$1,221.14	$243,949.63
24	$279.13	$1,219.75	$243,670.49
25	$280.53	$1,218.35	$243,389.97
26	$281.93	$1,216.95	$243,108.04
27	$283.34	$1,215.54	$242,824.70
28	$284.76	$1,214.12	$242,539.94

continued...

Payment	Principal	Interest	Balance
29	$286.18	$1,212.70	$242,253.76
30	$287.61	$1,211.27	$241,966.15
31	$289.05	$1,209.83	$241,677.10
32	$290.49	$1,208.39	$241,386.61
33	$291.95	$1,206.93	$241,094.66
34	$293.41	$1,205.47	$240,801.25
35	$294.87	$1,204.01	$240,506.38
36	$296.35	$1,202.53	$240,210.03
37	$297.83	$1,201.05	$239,912.20
38	$299.32	$1,199.56	$239,612.88
39	$300.82	$1,198.06	$239,312.07
40	$302.32	$1,196.56	$239,009.75
41	$303.83	$1,195.05	$238,705.91
42	$305.35	$1,193.53	$238,400.56
43	$306.88	$1,192.00	$238,093.69
44	$308.41	$1,190.47	$237,785.28
45	$309.95	$1,188.93	$237,475.32
46	$311.50	$1,187.38	$237,163.82
47	$313.06	$1,185.82	$236,850.76
48	$314.63	$1,184.25	$236,536.13
49	$316.20	$1,182.68	$236,219.93
50	$317.78	$1,181.10	$235,902.15
51	$319.37	$1,179.51	$235,582.78
52	$320.97	$1,177.91	$235,261.82
53	$322.57	$1,176.31	$234,939.25
54	$324.18	$1,174.70	$234,615.06
55	$325.80	$1,173.08	$234,289.26
56	$327.43	$1,171.45	$233,961.82
57	$329.07	$1,169.81	$233,632.75
58	$330.72	$1,168.16	$233,302.04
59	$332.37	$1,166.51	$232,969.67
60	$334.03	$1,164.85	$232,635.63

First Five Years of a 6.5%, 30-year Loan

Principal	Payment	APR	Total Interest	Total Loan Value
$250,000.00	$1,580.17	6.5000%	$318,861.20	$568,861.20

Payment	Principal	Interest	Balance
1	$226.00	$1,354.17	$249,774.00
2	$227.23	$1,352.94	$249,546.77
3	$228.46	$1,351.71	$249,318.31
4	$229.70	$1,350.47	$249,088.61
5	$230.94	$1,349.23	$248,857.67
6	$232.19	$1,347.98	$248,625.48
7	$233.45	$1,346.72	$248,392.04
8	$234.71	$1,345.46	$248,157.32
9	$235.98	$1,344.19	$247,921.34
10	$237.26	$1,342.91	$247,684.08
11	$238.55	$1,341.62	$247,445.53
12	$239.84	$1,340.33	$247,205.69
13	$241.14	$1,339.03	$246,964.55
14	$242.45	$1,337.72	$246,722.10
15	$243.76	$1,336.41	$246,478.34
16	$245.08	$1,335.09	$246,233.26
17	$246.41	$1,333.76	$245,986.86
18	$247.74	$1,332.43	$245,739.12
19	$249.08	$1,331.09	$245,490.03
20	$250.43	$1,329.74	$245,239.60
21	$251.79	$1,328.38	$244,987.81
22	$253.15	$1,327.02	$244,734.66
23	$254.52	$1,325.65	$244,480.14
24	$255.90	$1,324.27	$244,224.23
25	$257.29	$1,322.88	$243,966.95
26	$258.68	$1,321.49	$243,708.26
27	$260.08	$1,320.09	$243,448.18
28	$261.49	$1,318.68	$243,186.69

continued...

Payment	Principal	Interest	Balance
29	$262.91	$1,317.26	$242,923.78
30	$264.33	$1,315.84	$242,659.45
31	$265.76	$1,314.41	$242,393.68
32	$267.20	$1,312.97	$242,126.48
33	$268.65	$1,311.52	$241,857.82
34	$270.11	$1,310.06	$241,587.72
35	$271.57	$1,308.60	$241,316.15
36	$273.04	$1,307.13	$241,043.11
37	$274.52	$1,305.65	$240,768.59
38	$276.01	$1,304.16	$240,492.58
39	$277.50	$1,302.67	$240,215.08
40	$279.00	$1,301.17	$239,936.07
41	$280.52	$1,299.65	$239,655.56
42	$282.04	$1,298.13	$239,373.52
43	$283.56	$1,296.61	$239,089.96
44	$285.10	$1,295.07	$238,804.86
45	$286.64	$1,293.53	$238,518.22
46	$288.20	$1,291.97	$238,230.02
47	$289.76	$1,290.41	$237,940.26
48	$291.33	$1,288.84	$237,648.93
49	$292.90	$1,287.27	$237,356.03
50	$294.49	$1,285.68	$237,061.54
51	$296.09	$1,284.08	$236,765.45
52	$297.69	$1,282.48	$236,467.76
53	$299.30	$1,280.87	$236,168.46
54	$300.92	$1,279.25	$235,867.53
55	$302.55	$1,277.62	$235,564.98
56	$304.19	$1,275.98	$235,260.79
57	$305.84	$1,274.33	$234,954.95
58	$307.50	$1,272.67	$234,647.45
59	$309.16	$1,271.01	$234,338.29
60	$310.84	$1,269.33	$234,027.45

First Five Years of a 7%, 30-year Loan

Principal	Payment	APR	Total Interest	Total Loan Value
$250,000.00	$1,663.26	7.0000%	$348,773.60	$598,773.60

Payment	Principal	Interest	Balance
1	$204.93	$1,458.33	$249,795.07
2	$206.12	$1,457.14	$249,588.95
3	$207.32	$1,455.94	$249,381.63
4	$208.53	$1,454.73	$249,173.09
5	$209.75	$1,453.51	$248,963.34
6	$210.97	$1,452.29	$248,752.37
7	$212.20	$1,451.06	$248,540.16
8	$213.44	$1,449.82	$248,326.72
9	$214.69	$1,448.57	$248,112.03
10	$215.94	$1,447.32	$247,896.09
11	$217.20	$1,446.06	$247,678.90
12	$218.47	$1,444.79	$247,460.43
13	$219.74	$1,443.52	$247,240.69
14	$221.02	$1,442.24	$247,019.67
15	$222.31	$1,440.95	$246,797.35
16	$223.61	$1,439.65	$246,573.74
17	$224.91	$1,438.35	$246,348.83
18	$226.23	$1,437.03	$246,122.61
19	$227.54	$1,435.72	$245,895.06
20	$228.87	$1,434.39	$245,666.19
21	$230.21	$1,433.05	$245,435.98
22	$231.55	$1,431.71	$245,204.43
23	$232.90	$1,430.36	$244,971.53
24	$234.26	$1,429.00	$244,737.27
25	$235.63	$1,427.63	$244,501.65
26	$237.00	$1,426.26	$244,264.65
27	$238.38	$1,424.88	$244,026.26
28	$239.77	$1,423.49	$243,786.49

continued...

Payment	Principal	Interest	Balance
29	$241.17	$1,422.09	$243,545.32
30	$242.58	$1,420.68	$243,302.74
31	$243.99	$1,419.27	$243,058.74
32	$245.42	$1,417.84	$242,813.33
33	$246.85	$1,416.41	$242,566.48
34	$248.29	$1,414.97	$242,318.19
35	$249.74	$1,413.52	$242,068.45
36	$251.19	$1,412.07	$241,817.26
37	$252.66	$1,410.60	$241,564.60
38	$254.13	$1,409.13	$241,310.47
39	$255.62	$1,407.64	$241,054.85
40	$257.11	$1,406.15	$240,797.74
41	$258.61	$1,404.65	$240,539.14
42	$260.12	$1,403.14	$240,279.02
43	$261.63	$1,401.63	$240,017.39
44	$263.16	$1,400.10	$239,754.23
45	$264.69	$1,398.57	$239,489.54
46	$266.24	$1,397.02	$239,223.30
47	$267.79	$1,395.47	$238,955.51
48	$269.35	$1,393.91	$238,686.16
49	$270.92	$1,392.34	$238,415.23
50	$272.50	$1,390.76	$238,142.73
51	$274.09	$1,389.17	$237,868.63
52	$275.69	$1,387.57	$237,592.94
53	$277.30	$1,385.96	$237,315.64
54	$278.92	$1,384.34	$237,036.72
55	$280.55	$1,382.71	$236,756.17
56	$282.18	$1,381.08	$236,473.99
57	$283.83	$1,379.43	$236,190.16
58	$285.48	$1,377.78	$235,904.68
59	$287.15	$1,376.11	$235,617.53
60	$288.82	$1,374.44	$235,328.71

First Five Years of a 6%, 15-year Loan

Principal	Payment	APR	Total Interest	Total Loan Value
$250,000.00	$2,109.64	6.0000%	$129,735.20	$379,735.20

Payment	Principal	Interest	Balance
1	$859.64	$1,250.00	$249,140.36
2	$863.94	$1,245.70	$248,276.42
3	$868.26	$1,241.38	$247,408.16
4	$872.60	$1,237.04	$246,535.56
5	$876.96	$1,232.68	$245,658.60
6	$881.35	$1,228.29	$244,777.26
7	$885.75	$1,223.89	$243,891.50
8	$890.18	$1,219.46	$243,001.32
9	$894.63	$1,215.01	$242,106.69
10	$899.11	$1,210.53	$241,207.58
11	$903.60	$1,206.04	$240,303.98
12	$908.12	$1,201.52	$239,395.86
13	$912.66	$1,196.98	$238,483.20
14	$917.22	$1,192.42	$237,565.97
15	$921.81	$1,187.83	$236,644.16
16	$926.42	$1,183.22	$235,717.74
17	$931.05	$1,178.59	$234,786.69
18	$935.71	$1,173.93	$233,850.99
19	$940.39	$1,169.25	$232,910.60
20	$945.09	$1,164.55	$231,965.51
21	$949.81	$1,159.83	$231,015.70
22	$954.56	$1,155.08	$230,061.14
23	$959.33	$1,150.31	$229,101.80
24	$964.13	$1,145.51	$228,137.67
25	$968.95	$1,140.69	$227,168.72
26	$973.80	$1,135.84	$226,194.93
27	$978.67	$1,130.97	$225,216.26
28	$983.56	$1,126.08	$224,232.70

continued...

Payment	Principal	Interest	Balance
29	$988.48	$1,121.16	$223,244.23
30	$993.42	$1,116.22	$222,250.81
31	$998.39	$1,111.25	$221,252.42
32	$1,003.38	$1,106.26	$220,249.04
33	$1,008.39	$1,101.25	$219,240.65
34	$1,013.44	$1,096.20	$218,227.21
35	$1,018.50	$1,091.14	$217,208.71
36	$1,023.60	$1,086.04	$216,185.11
37	$1,028.71	$1,080.93	$215,156.40
38	$1,033.86	$1,075.78	$214,122.54
39	$1,039.03	$1,070.61	$213,083.51
40	$1,044.22	$1,065.42	$212,039.29
41	$1,049.44	$1,060.20	$210,989.84
42	$1,054.69	$1,054.95	$209,935.15
43	$1,059.96	$1,049.68	$208,875.19
44	$1,065.26	$1,044.38	$207,809.93
45	$1,070.59	$1,039.05	$206,739.34
46	$1,075.94	$1,033.70	$205,663.39
47	$1,081.32	$1,028.32	$204,582.07
48	$1,086.73	$1,022.91	$203,495.34
49	$1,092.16	$1,017.48	$202,403.18
50	$1,097.62	$1,012.02	$201,305.55
51	$1,103.11	$1,006.53	$200,202.44
52	$1,108.63	$1,001.01	$199,093.81
53	$1,114.17	$995.47	$197,979.64
54	$1,119.74	$989.90	$196,859.90
55	$1,125.34	$984.30	$195,734.56
56	$1,130.97	$978.67	$194,603.59
57	$1,136.62	$973.02	$193,466.97
58	$1,142.31	$967.33	$192,324.66
59	$1,148.02	$961.62	$191,176.65
60	$1,153.76	$955.88	$190,022.89

First Five Years of a 6.5%, 15-year Loan

Principal	Payment	APR	Total Interest	Total Loan Value
$250,000.00	$2,177.77	6.5000%	$141,998.60	$391,998.60

Payment	Principal	Interest	Balance
1	$823.60	$1,354.17	$249,176.40
2	$828.06	$1,349.71	$248,348.33
3	$832.55	$1,345.22	$247,515.78
4	$837.06	$1,340.71	$246,678.72
5	$841.59	$1,336.18	$245,837.13
6	$846.15	$1,331.62	$244,990.98
7	$850.74	$1,327.03	$244,140.24
8	$855.34	$1,322.43	$243,284.90
9	$859.98	$1,317.79	$242,424.92
10	$864.64	$1,313.13	$241,560.29
11	$869.32	$1,308.45	$240,690.97
12	$874.03	$1,303.74	$239,816.94
13	$878.76	$1,299.01	$238,938.18
14	$883.52	$1,294.25	$238,054.66
15	$888.31	$1,289.46	$237,166.35
16	$893.12	$1,284.65	$236,273.23
17	$897.96	$1,279.81	$235,375.27
18	$902.82	$1,274.95	$234,472.45
19	$907.71	$1,270.06	$233,564.74
20	$912.63	$1,265.14	$232,652.12
21	$917.57	$1,260.20	$231,734.54
22	$922.54	$1,255.23	$230,812.00
23	$927.54	$1,250.23	$229,884.46
24	$932.56	$1,245.21	$228,951.90
25	$937.61	$1,240.16	$228,014.29
26	$942.69	$1,235.08	$227,071.60
27	$947.80	$1,229.97	$226,123.80
28	$952.93	$1,224.84	$225,170.86

continued...

Payment	Principal	Interest	Balance
29	$958.09	$1,219.68	$224,212.77
30	$963.28	$1,214.49	$223,249.49
31	$968.50	$1,209.27	$222,280.98
32	$973.75	$1,204.02	$221,307.24
33	$979.02	$1,198.75	$220,328.21
34	$984.33	$1,193.44	$219,343.89
35	$989.66	$1,188.11	$218,354.23
36	$995.02	$1,182.75	$217,359.21
37	$1,000.41	$1,177.36	$216,358.80
38	$1,005.83	$1,171.94	$215,352.98
39	$1,011.27	$1,166.50	$214,341.70
40	$1,016.75	$1,161.02	$213,324.95
41	$1,022.26	$1,155.51	$212,302.69
42	$1,027.80	$1,149.97	$211,274.89
43	$1,033.36	$1,144.41	$210,241.53
44	$1,038.96	$1,138.81	$209,202.57
45	$1,044.59	$1,133.18	$208,157.98
46	$1,050.25	$1,127.52	$207,107.73
47	$1,055.94	$1,121.83	$206,051.79
48	$1,061.66	$1,116.11	$204,990.14
49	$1,067.41	$1,110.36	$203,922.73
50	$1,073.19	$1,104.58	$202,849.54
51	$1,079.00	$1,098.77	$201,770.54
52	$1,084.85	$1,092.92	$200,685.70
53	$1,090.72	$1,087.05	$199,594.97
54	$1,096.63	$1,081.14	$198,498.34
55	$1,102.57	$1,075.20	$197,395.77
56	$1,108.54	$1,069.23	$196,287.23
57	$1,114.55	$1,063.22	$195,172.68
58	$1,120.58	$1,057.19	$194,052.10
59	$1,126.65	$1,051.12	$192,925.44
60	$1,132.76	$1,045.01	$191,792.68

First Five Years on a 7%, 15-year Loan

Principal	Payment	APR	Total Interest	Total Loan Value
$250,000.00	$2,247.07	7.0000%	$154,472.60	$404,472.60

Payment	Principal	Interest	Balance
1	$788.74	$1,458.33	$249,211.26
2	$793.34	$1,453.73	$248,417.93
3	$797.97	$1,449.10	$247,619.96
4	$802.62	$1,444.45	$246,817.34
5	$807.30	$1,439.77	$246,010.04
6	$812.01	$1,435.06	$245,198.03
7	$816.75	$1,430.32	$244,381.28
8	$821.51	$1,425.56	$243,559.77
9	$826.30	$1,420.77	$242,733.46
10	$831.12	$1,415.95	$241,902.34
11	$835.97	$1,411.10	$241,066.36
12	$840.85	$1,406.22	$240,225.51
13	$845.75	$1,401.32	$239,379.76
14	$850.69	$1,396.38	$238,529.07
15	$855.65	$1,391.42	$237,673.42
16	$860.64	$1,386.43	$236,812.78
17	$865.66	$1,381.41	$235,947.12
18	$870.71	$1,376.36	$235,076.40
19	$875.79	$1,371.28	$234,200.61
20	$880.90	$1,366.17	$233,319.71
21	$886.04	$1,361.03	$232,433.68
22	$891.21	$1,355.86	$231,542.47
23	$896.41	$1,350.66	$230,646.06
24	$901.63	$1,345.44	$229,744.43
25	$906.89	$1,340.18	$228,837.53
26	$912.18	$1,334.89	$227,925.35
27	$917.51	$1,329.56	$227,007.84
28	$922.86	$1,324.21	$226,084.99

continued...

Payment	Principal	Interest	Balance
29	$928.24	$1,318.83	$225,156.75
30	$933.66	$1,313.41	$224,223.09
31	$939.10	$1,307.97	$223,283.99
32	$944.58	$1,302.49	$222,339.41
33	$950.09	$1,296.98	$221,389.32
34	$955.63	$1,291.44	$220,433.69
35	$961.21	$1,285.86	$219,472.48
36	$966.81	$1,280.26	$218,505.67
37	$972.45	$1,274.62	$217,533.21
38	$978.13	$1,268.94	$216,555.09
39	$983.83	$1,263.24	$215,571.25
40	$989.57	$1,257.50	$214,581.68
41	$995.34	$1,251.73	$213,586.34
42	$1,001.15	$1,245.92	$212,585.19
43	$1,006.99	$1,240.08	$211,578.20
44	$1,012.86	$1,234.21	$210,565.34
45	$1,018.77	$1,228.30	$209,546.56
46	$1,024.72	$1,222.35	$208,521.85
47	$1,030.69	$1,216.38	$207,491.16
48	$1,036.70	$1,210.37	$206,454.45
49	$1,042.75	$1,204.32	$205,411.70
50	$1,048.84	$1,198.23	$204,362.86
51	$1,054.95	$1,192.12	$203,307.91
52	$1,061.11	$1,185.96	$202,246.80
53	$1,067.30	$1,179.77	$201,179.51
54	$1,073.52	$1,173.55	$200,105.98
55	$1,079.79	$1,167.28	$199,026.20
56	$1,086.08	$1,160.99	$197,940.11
57	$1,092.42	$1,154.65	$196,847.69
58	$1,098.79	$1,148.28	$195,748.90
59	$1,105.20	$1,141.87	$194,643.70
60	$1,111.65	$1,135.42	$193,532.05

First Five Years of 7% 30-year Loan
with Additional $100/month Payment

Month	(Year)	Balance	Payment	Interest	Paid Principal
1	0.08	249,695.07	1,763.26	1,458.33	304.93
2	0.17	249,388.37	1,763.26	1,456.55	306.71
3	0.25	249,079.87	1,763.26	1,454.77	308.49
4	0.33	248,769.58	1,763.26	1,452.97	310.29
5	0.42	248,457.48	1,763.26	1,451.16	312.10
6	0.50	248,143.55	1,763.26	1,449.34	313.92
7	0.58	247,827.79	1,763.26	1,447.50	315.76
8	0.67	247,510.20	1,763.26	1,445.66	317.60
9	0.75	247,190.75	1,763.26	1,443.81	319.45
10	0.83	246,869.43	1,763.26	1,441.95	321.31
11	0.92	246,546.24	1,763.26	1,440.07	323.19
12	1.00	246,221.17	1,763.26	1,438.19	325.07
13	1.08	245,894.20	1,763.26	1,436.29	326.97
14	1.17	245,565.32	1,763.26	1,434.38	328.88
15	1.25	245,234.53	1,763.26	1,432.46	330.80
16	1.33	244,901.80	1,763.26	1,430.53	332.73
17	1.42	244,567.14	1,763.26	1,428.59	334.67
18	1.50	244,230.52	1,763.26	1,426.64	336.62
19	1.58	243,891.94	1,763.26	1,424.68	338.58
20	1.67	243,551.38	1,763.26	1,422.70	340.56
21	1.75	243,208.84	1,763.26	1,420.72	342.54
22	1.83	242,864.29	1,763.26	1,418.72	344.54
23	1.92	242,517.74	1,763.26	1,416.71	346.55
24	2.00	242,169.17	1,763.26	1,414.69	348.57
25	2.08	241,818.56	1,763.26	1,412.65	350.61
26	2.17	241,465.91	1,763.26	1,410.61	352.65
27	2.25	241,111.20	1,763.26	1,408.55	354.71
28	2.33	240,754.42	1,763.26	1,406.48	356.78
29	2.42	240,395.56	1,763.26	1,404.40	358.86

continued...

Month	(Year)	Balance	Payment	Interest	Paid Principal
30	2.50	240,034.61	1,763.26	1,402.31	360.95
31	2.58	239,671.55	1,763.26	1,400.20	363.06
32	2.67	239,306.38	1,763.26	1,398.08	365.18
33	2.75	238,939.07	1,763.26	1,395.95	367.31
34	2.83	238,569.62	1,763.26	1,393.81	369.45
35	2.92	238,198.02	1,763.26	1,391.66	371.60
36	3.00	237,824.25	1,763.26	1,389.49	373.77
37	3.08	237,448.30	1,763.26	1,387.31	375.95
38	3.17	237,070.15	1,763.26	1,385.12	378.14
39	3.25	236,689.80	1,763.26	1,382.91	380.35
40	3.33	236,307.23	1,763.26	1,380.69	382.57
41	3.42	235,922.43	1,763.26	1,378.46	384.80
42	3.50	235,535.38	1,763.26	1,376.21	387.05
43	3.58	235,146.08	1,763.26	1,373.96	389.30
44	3.67	234,754.51	1,763.26	1,371.69	391.57
45	3.75	234,360.65	1,763.26	1,369.40	393.86
46	3.83	233,964.49	1,763.26	1,367.10	396.16
47	3.92	233,566.02	1,763.26	1,364.79	398.47
48	4.00	233,165.23	1,763.26	1,362.47	400.79
49	4.08	232,762.10	1,763.26	1,360.13	403.13
50	4.17	232,356.62	1,763.26	1,357.78	405.48
51	4.25	231,948.77	1,763.26	1,355.41	407.85
52	4.33	231,538.55	1,763.26	1,353.03	410.23
53	4.42	231,125.93	1,763.26	1,350.64	412.62
54	4.50	230,710.91	1,763.26	1,348.23	415.03
55	4.58	230,293.46	1,763.26	1,345.81	417.45
56	4.67	229,873.58	1,763.26	1,343.38	419.88
57	4.75	229,451.25	1,763.26	1,340.93	422.33
58	4.83	229,026.45	1,763.26	1,338.47	424.79
59	4.92	228,599.18	1,763.26	1,335.99	427.27
60	5.00	228,169.42	1,763.26	1,333.50	429.76

Home Ownership and Equity Protection Act

The following is an excerpt from the Federal Reserve explaining the reason for the *Home Ownership and Equity Protection Act* (HOEPA) and some of its provisions. This will give you a general understanding of the problems associated with unfair mortgage loan practices and what the government is doing to mitigate them.

Should you wish to contact the board, call the Division of Consumer and Community Affairs at 202-452-3667 or 202-452-2412.

I. Background

Since the mid-1990s, the sub-prime mortgage market has grown substantially, providing access to credit to borrowers with less-than-perfect credit histories and to other borrowers who are not served by prime lenders. With this increase in sub-prime lending, there has also been an increase in reports of predatory lending. The term *predatory lending* encompasses a variety of practices. In general, the term is used to refer to abusive lending practices involving fraud, deception, or unfairness. Some abusive practices are clearly unlawful, but others involve loan terms that are legitimate in many instances and abusive in others, and thus, are difficult to regulate.

Loan terms that may benefit some borrowers, such as balloon payments, may harm other borrowers—particularly if they are not fully aware of the consequences. The reports of predatory lending have generally included one or more of the following:

- making unaffordable loans based on the borrower's home equity without regard to the borrower's ability to repay the obligation;
- inducing a borrower to refinance a loan repeatedly, even though the refinancing may not be in the borrower's interest, and charging high points and fees each time the loan is refinanced, which decreases the consumer's equity in the home; and,
- engaging in fraud or deception to conceal the true nature of the loan obligation from an unsuspecting or unsophisticated borrower. For example, *packing* loans with credit insurance without a consumer's consent.

A. The Home Ownership and Equity Protection Act

In response to anecdotal evidence about abusive practices involving home-secured loans with high rates or high fees, in 1994 Congress enacted the *Home Ownership and Equity Protection Act* (HOEPA), Pub. L. 103-325, 108 Stat. 2160, as an amendment to the *Truth in Lending Act* (TILA), 15 U.S.C. 1601 et seq. TILA is intended to promote the informed use of consumer credit by requiring disclosures about its terms and cost. TILA requires creditors to disclose the cost of credit as a dollar amount (the *finance charge*) and as an annual percentage rate (APR).

Uniformity in creditors' disclosures is intended to assist consumers in comparison shopping. TILA requires additional disclosures for loans secured by a consumer's home and permits consumers to rescind certain transactions that involve their principal dwelling. TILA is implemented by the Board's *Regulation Z*, 12 CFR part 226. HOEPA identifies a class of high-cost mortgage loans through rate and fee triggers, and it provides consumers entering into these transactions with special protections. HOEPA applies to closed-end, home equity loans (excluding home-purchase loans) bearing rates or fees above a specified percentage or amount. A loan is covered by HOEPA if (1) the APR exceeds the rate for Treasury securities with a comparable maturity by more than 10 percentage points or (2) the points and fees paid by the consumer exceed the greater of 8 percent of the loan amount or $400. The $400 figure set in 1994 is adjusted annually based on the Consumer Price Index. The dollar figure for 2001 is $465 and for 2002

is $480. (66 FR 57849, November 19, 2001.) HOEPA is implemented in Sec. 226.32 of the Board's Regulation Z.

HOEPA also amended TILA to require additional disclosures for reverse mortgages that are contained in Sec. 226.33 of Regulation Z. For purposes of this notice of rulemaking, however, the term *HOEPA covered loan* (or *HOEPA loan*) refers only to mortgages covered by Sec. 226.32 that meet HOEPA's rate or fee-based triggers. Creditors offering HOEPA covered loans must give consumers an abbreviated disclosure statement at least three business days before the loan is closed, in addition to the disclosures generally required by TILA before or at closing. The HOEPA disclosure informs consumers that they are not obligated to complete the transaction and could lose their home if they take the loan and fail to make payments. It includes a few key items of cost information, including the APR. In loans where consumers have three business days after closing to rescind the loan, the HOEPA disclosure thus affords consumers a minimum of six business days to consider accepting key loan terms before receiving the loan proceeds. HOEPA restricts certain loan terms for high-cost loans because they are associated with abusive lending practices. These terms include short-term balloon notes, prepayment penalties, non-amortizing payment schedules, and higher interest rates upon default. Creditors are prohibited from engaging in a pattern or practice of making HOEPA loans based on the homeowner's equity without regard to the borrower's ability to repay the loan. Under HOEPA, assignees are generally subject to all claims and defenses with respect to a HOEPA loan that a consumer could assert against the creditor. HOEPA also authorizes the Board to prohibit acts or practices in connection with mortgage lending under defined criteria.

Section 1602 (aa)

(1) A mortgage referred to in this subsection means a consumer credit transaction that is secured by the consumer's principal dwelling, other than a residential mortgage transaction, a reverse mortgage transaction, or a transaction under an open end credit plan, if —

(A) the annual percentage rate at consummation of the transaction will exceed by more than 10 percentage points the yield on Treasury securities having comparable periods of maturity on the fifteenth day of the month immediately preceding the month in which the application for the extension of credit is received by the creditor; or

(B) the total points and fees payable by the consumer at or before closing will exceed the greater of —

(i) 8 percent of the total loan amount; or

(ii) $400.

(a) Disclosures
(1) Specific disclosures

In addition to other disclosures required under this subchapter, for each mortgage referred to in section 1602 (aa) of this title, the creditor shall provide the following disclosures in conspicuous type size:

(A) "You are not required to complete this agreement merely because you have received these disclosures or have signed a loan application."

(B) "If you obtain this loan, the lender will have a mortgage on your home. You could lose your home, and any money you have put into it, if you do not meet your obligations under the loan."

(2) Annual percentage rate

In addition to the disclosures required under paragraph (1), the creditor shall disclose —

(A) in the case of a credit transaction with a fixed rate of interest, the annual percentage rate and the amount of the regular monthly payment; or

(B) in the case of any other credit transaction, the annual percentage rate of the loan, the amount of the regular monthly payment, a statement that the interest rate and monthly payment may increase, and the amount of the maximum monthly payment, based on the maximum interest rate allowed pursuant to section 3806 of title 12.

(b) Time of disclosures
(1) In general
The disclosures required by this section shall be given not less than 3 business days prior to consummation of the transaction.
(2) New disclosures required
(A) In general
After providing the disclosures required by this section, a creditor may not change the terms of the extension of credit if such changes make the disclosures inaccurate, unless new disclosures are provided that meet the requirements of this section.

(B) Telephone disclosure
A creditor may provide new disclosures pursuant to subparagraph (A) by telephone, if —
(i) the change is initiated by the consumer; and
(ii) at the consummation of the transaction under which the credit is extended —
(I) the creditor provides to the consumer the new disclosures, in writing; and
(II) the creditor and consumer certify in writing that the new disclosures were provided by telephone, by not later than 3 days prior to the date of consummation of the transaction.

(3) Modifications
The Board may, if it finds that such action is necessary to permit home-owners to meet bona fide personal financial emergencies, prescribe regulations authorizing the modification or waiver of rights created under this subsection, to the extent and under the circumstances set forth in those regulations.

(c) No Prepayment penalty
(1) In general
(A) Limitation on terms

A mortgage referred to in section 1602 (aa) of this title may not contain terms under which a consumer must pay a prepayment penalty for paying all or part of the principal before the date on which the principal is due.

(B) Construction

For purposes of this subsection, any method of computing a refund of unearned scheduled interest is a prepayment penalty if it is less favorable to the consumer than the actuarial method (as that term is defined in section 1615 (d) of this title).

(2) Exception

Notwithstanding paragraph (1), a mortgage referred to in section 1602 (aa) of this title may contain a prepayment penalty (including terms calculating a refund by a method that is not prohibited under section 1615 (b) of this title for the transaction in question) if —

(A) at the time the mortgage is consummated —

(i) the consumer is not liable for an amount of monthly indebtedness payments (including the amount of credit extended or to be extended under the transaction) that is greater than 50 percent of the monthly gross income of the consumer; and

(ii) the income and expenses of the consumer are verified by a financial statement signed by the consumer, by a credit report, and in the case of employment income, by payment records or by verification from the employer of the consumer (which verification may be in the form of a copy of a pay stub or other payment record supplied by the consumer);

(B) the penalty applies only to a prepayment made with amounts obtained by the consumer by means other than a refinancing by the creditor under the mortgage, or an affiliate of that creditor;

(C) the penalty does not apply after the end of the 5-year period beginning on the date on which the mortgage is consummated; and,

(D) the penalty is not prohibited under other applicable law.

(d) Limitations after default

A mortgage referred to in section 1602 (aa) of this title may not provide for an interest rate applicable after default that is higher than the interest rate that applies before default. If the date of maturity of a mortgage referred to in subsection [1] 1602(aa) of this title is accelerated due to default and the consumer is entitled to a rebate of interest, that rebate shall be computed by any method that is not less favorable than the actuarial method (as that term is defined in section 1615 (d) of this title).

(e) No balloon payments

A mortgage referred to in section 1602 (aa) of this title having a term of less than 5 years may not include terms under which the aggregate amount of the regular periodic payments would not fully amortize the outstanding principal balance.

(f) No negative amortization

A mortgage referred to in section 1602 (aa) of this title may not include terms under which the outstanding principal balance will increase at any time over the course of the loan because the regular periodic payments do not cover the full amount of interest due.

(g) No prepaid payments

A mortgage referred to in section 1602 (aa) of this title may not include terms under which more than 2 periodic payments required under the loan are consolidated and paid in advance from the loan proceeds provided to the consumer.

(h) Prohibition on extending credit without regard to payment ability of consumer

A creditor shall not engage in a pattern or practice of extending credit to consumers under mortgages referred to in section 1602 (aa) of this title based on the consumers' collateral without regard to the consumers' repayment ability, including the consumers' current and expected income, current obligations, and employment.

The Real Estate Settlement Procedures Act

The *Real Estate Settlement Procedures Act* (RESPA) is enforced by the U.S. Department of Housing and Urban Development (HUD). HUD defines the Act as follows.

> *RESPA is about closing costs and settlement procedures. RESPA is a HUD consumer protection statute designed to help homebuyers be better shoppers in the home buying process. RESPA requires that consumers receive disclosures at various times in the transaction and outlaws kickbacks that increase the cost of settlement services.*

A visit to the HUD website gives much valuable information both as to your rights and how to file a complaint if you believe your lender is not following the law. There is also information on mortgage insurance and consumer tips.

The site also contains a frequently asked questions section that has several examples of what is not protected by RESPA. It is worthwhile reading before filing a complaint.

The following information modified from the RESPA website gives a more detailed explanation of some of RESPA's requirements.

RESPA requires that borrowers receive disclosures at various times. Some disclosures spell out the costs associated with the settlement, outline lender servicing and escrow account practices, and describe business relationships between settlement service providers.

RESPA also prohibits certain practices that increase the cost of settlement services. Section 8 of RESPA prohibits a person from giving or accepting anything of value for referrals of settlement service business related to a federally related mortgage loan. It also prohibits a person from giving or accepting any part of a charge for services that are not performed. Section 9 of RESPA prohibits home sellers from requiring home buyers to purchase title insurance from a particular company.

RESPA covers loans secured with a mortgage placed on a one-to-four family residential property. These include most purchase loans, assumptions, refinances, property improvement loans, and equity lines of credit. HUD's Office of RESPA and Interstate Land Sales is responsible for enforcing RESPA.

RESPA Required Disclosures

At the Time of Loan Application—

When borrowers apply for a mortgage loan, mortgage brokers and/or lenders must give the borrowers the following.

- A Special Information Booklet, which contains consumer information regarding various real estate settlement services. (Required for purchase transactions only.)
- A Good Faith Estimate (GFE) of settlement costs, which lists the charges the buyer is likely to pay at settlement. This is only an estimate and the actual charges may differ. If a lender requires the borrower to use of a particular settlement provider, then the lender must disclose this requirement on the GFE.
- A Mortgage Servicing Disclosure Statement, which discloses to the borrower whether the lender intends to service the loan or transfer it to another lender. It also provides information about complaint resolution.

If the borrowers do not get these documents at the time of application, the lender must mail them within three business days of receiving the loan application.

If the lender turns down the loan within three days, however, then RESPA does not require the lender to provide these documents.

The RESPA statute does not provide an explicit penalty for the failure to provide the Special Information Booklet, Good Faith Estimate or Mortgage Servicing Statement. However, bank regulators may choose to impose penalties on lenders who fail to comply with federal law. Please read the section on RESPA enforcement for more information.

Disclosures before Settlement/Closing Occurs—

NOTE: *The terms settlement and closing can be and are used interchangeably.*

An *Affiliated Business Arrangement* (AfBA) *Disclosure* is required whenever a settlement service provider involved in a RESPA covered transaction refers the consumer to a provider with whom the referring party has an ownership or other beneficial interest.

The referring party must give the AfBA disclosure to the consumer at or prior to the time of referral. The disclosure must describe the business arrangement that exists between the two providers and give the borrower an estimate of the second provider's charges.

Except in cases where a lender refers a borrower to an attorney, credit reporting agency or real estate appraiser to represent the lender's interest in the transaction, the referring party may not require the consumer to use the particular provider being referred.

The *HUD-1 Settlement Statement* is a standard form that clearly shows all charges imposed on borrowers and sellers in connection with the settlement. RESPA allows the borrower to request to see the HUD-1 Settlement Statement one day before the actual settlement. The settlement agent must then provide the borrowers with a completed HUD-1 Settlement Statement based on information known to the agent at that time.

Disclosures at Settlement—

The HUD-1 Settlement Statement shows the actual settlement costs of the loan transaction. Separate forms may be prepared for the borrower and

the seller. Where it is not the practice that the borrower and the seller both attend the settlement, the HUD-1 should be mailed or delivered as soon as practicable after settlement.

The *Initial Escrow Statement* itemizes the estimated taxes, insurance premiums and other charges anticipated to be paid from the Escrow Account during the first twelve months of the loan. It lists the Escrow payment amount and any required cushion. Although the statement is usually given at settlement, the lender has 45 days from settlement to deliver it.

Disclosures after Settlement—

Loan servicers must deliver to borrowers an *Annual Escrow Statement* once a year. The annual escrow account statement summarizes all escrow account deposits and payments during the servicer's twelve month computation year. It also notifies the borrower of any shortages or surpluses in the account and advises the borrower about the course of action being taken.

A *Servicing Transfer Statement* is required if the loan servicer sells or assigns the servicing rights to a borrower's loan to another loan servicer. Generally, the loan servicer must notify the borrower 15 days before the effective date of the loan transfer. As long as the borrower makes a timely payment to the old servicer within 60 days of the loan transfer, the borrower cannot be penalized. The notice must include the name and address of the new servicer, toll-free telephone numbers, and the date the new servicer will begin accepting payments.

RESPA's: Consumer Protections and Prohibited Practices

Section 8: Kickbacks, Fee-Splitting, Unearned Fees

Section 8 of RESPA prohibits anyone from giving or accepting a fee, kickback or any thing of value in exchange for referrals of settlement service business

involving a federally related mortgage loan. In addition, RESPA prohibits fee splitting and receiving unearned fees for services not actually performed.

Violations of Section 8's anti-kickback, referral fees and unearned fees provisions of RESPA are subject to criminal and civil penalties. In a criminal case a person who violates Section 8 may be fined up to $10,000 and imprisoned up to one year. In a private law suit, a person who violates Section 8 may be liable to the person charged for the settlement service an amount equal to three times the amount of the charge paid for the service.

Section 9: Seller Required Title Insurance

Section 9 of RESPA prohibits a seller from requiring the home buyer to use a particular title insurance company, either directly or indirectly, as a condition of sale. Buyers may sue a seller who violates this provision for an amount equal to three times all charges made for the title insurance.

Section 10: Limits on Escrow Accounts

Section 10 of RESPA sets limits on the amounts that a lender may require a borrower to put into an escrow account for purposes of paying taxes, hazard insurance and other charges related to the property. RESPA does not require lenders to impose an escrow account on borrowers; however, certain government loan programs or lenders may require escrow accounts as a condition of the loan.

During the course of the loan, RESPA prohibits a lender from charging excessive amounts for the escrow account. Each month, the lender may require a borrower to pay into the escrow account no more than $\frac{1}{12}$ of the total of all disbursements payable during the year, plus an amount necessary to pay for any shortage in the account. In addition, the lender may require a cushion, not to exceed an amount equal to $\frac{1}{6}$ of the total disbursements for the year.

The lender must perform an escrow account analysis once during the year and notify borrowers of any shortage. Any excess of $50 or more must be returned to the borrower.

RESPA Enforcement

Civil Law Suits

Individuals have one (1) year to bring a private law suit to enforce violations of Section 8 or 9. A person may bring an action for violations of Section 6 within three years. Lawsuits for violations of Section 6, 8, or 9 may be brought in any federal district court in the district in which the property is located or where the violation is alleged to have occurred.

HUD, a State Attorney General or State insurance commissioner may bring an injunctive action to enforce violations of Section 6, 8, or 9 of RESPA within three (3) years.

Loan Servicing Complaints

Section 6 provides borrowers with important consumer protections relating to the servicing of their loans. Under Section 6 of RESPA, borrowers who have a problem with the servicing of their loan (including escrow account questions), should contact their loan servicer in writing, outlining the nature of their complaint. The servicer must acknowledge the complaint in writing within 20 business days of receipt of the complaint. Within 60 business days the servicer must resolve the complaint by correcting the account or giving a statement of the reasons for its position. Until the complaint is resolved, borrowers should continue to make the servicer's required payment.

A borrower may bring a private law suit, or a group of borrowers may bring a class action suit, within three years, against a servicer who fails to comply with Section 6's provisions. Borrowers may obtain actual damages, as well as additional damages if there is a pattern of noncompliance.

Other Enforcement Actions

Under Section 10, HUD has authority to impose a civil penalty on loan servicers who do not submit initial or annual escrow account statements to borrowers. Borrowers should contact HUD's Office of Consumer and

Regulatory Affairs to report servicers who fail to provide the required escrow account statements.

Filing a RESPA Complaint

Persons who believe a settlement service provider has violated RESPA in an area in which the Department has enforcement authority (primarily sections 6, 8, and 9) may wish to file a complaint. The complaint should outline the violation and identify the violators by name, address, and phone number. Complainants should also provide their own name and phone number for follow up questions from HUD. Requests for confidentiality will be honored. Complaints should be sent to:

Director, Office of RESPA and Interstate Land Sales
U.S. Department of Housing and Urban Development
Room 9154
451 7th Street, S.W.
Washington, DC 20410

Index

D

E

About the Author

John J. Talamo has a long and distinguished career as an attorney in Orange County, California. He graduated from the University of Notre Dame and received his law degree from the Detroit College of Law at Michigan State University.

In addition to advising clients on all matters relating to buying, selling, owning, and renting property, Mr. Talamo has written or coauthored several book on topics relating to real estate. Some of these titles include *The Landlord's Legal Guide in California*, *Tenants' Rights in California*, and *The Real Estate Dictionary*, which has sold over two million copies and is used nationally by government agencies, title companies, escrow companies, and real estate agents.

He has taught real estate courses for years and is currently splitting his time between the booming real estate markets of Southern California and outside Las Vegas, Nevada.

Copyright © 2005 by John Talamo
Cover and internal design © 2005 by Sourcebooks, Inc.®

First Edition: 2005
Second Printing: June, 2005

Published by: Sphinx® Publishing, An Imprint of Sourcebooks, Inc.®

Naperville Office
P.O. Box 4410
Naperville, Illinois 60567-4410
630-961-3900
Fax: 630-961-2168
www.sourcebooks.com
www.SphinxLegal.com

This publication is designed to provide accurate and authoritative information in regard to the subject matter covered. It is sold with the understanding that the publisher is not engaged in rendering legal, accounting, or other professional service. If legal advice or other expert assistance is required, the services of a competent professional person should be sought.

From a Declaration of Principles Jointly Adopted by a Committee of the American Bar Association and a Committee of Publishers and Associations

This product is not a substitute for legal advice.

Disclaimer required by Texas statutes.

Library of Congress Cataloging-in-Publication Data
Talamo, John.
  The mortgage answer book : choosing the right loan for you / by John J. Talamo.-- 1st ed.
    p. cm.
  ISBN 1-57248-480-2 (pbk. : alk. paper)
  1. Mortgage loans--United States. I. Title.
  HG2040.5.U5T35 2005
  332.7'22'0973--dc22
                              2005004892

Printed and bound in the United States of America.

BG 10 9 8 7 6 5 4 3 2

M

Choo

SPHINX PUBLISHING
AN IMPRINT OF SOURCEBOOKS, INC.®
NAPERVILLE, ILLINOIS
www.SphinxLegal.com